BEST TEA SHOP WALKS IN CHESHIRE

Clive Price

Published by Sigma Leisure – an imprint of
Sigma Press, 5 Alton Road, Wilmslow, Cheshire SK9 5DY, England.

British Library Cataloguing in Publication Data
A CIP record for this book is available from the British Library.

ISBN: 1-85058-809-0

Typesetting and Design by: Sigma Press, Wilmslow, Cheshire.

Cover: The Penny Farthing Museum and Courtyard Coffee House, Knutsford *(Chris Rushton)*

Maps: Jeremy Semmens

Photographs: the author

Printed by: Bell & Bain Ltd., Glasgow

Acknowledgements: My thanks are due to Frank McGowan who has acted as chauffeur on several occasions. Considerable assistance has been provided by members of the Tourism and Marketing Unit and the Countryside Service of Cheshire County Council, and also the staff in the Tourist Information Centres in Chester, Nantwich, Ellesmere Port and Knutsford. Finally, I must mention the enormous support provided by my family.

Contents

The Walks

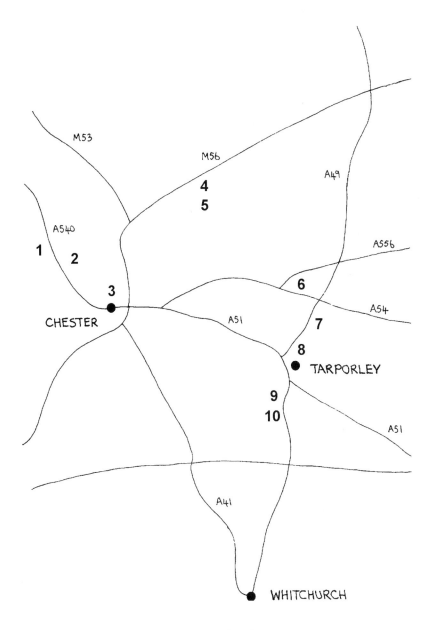

Location Map (1)

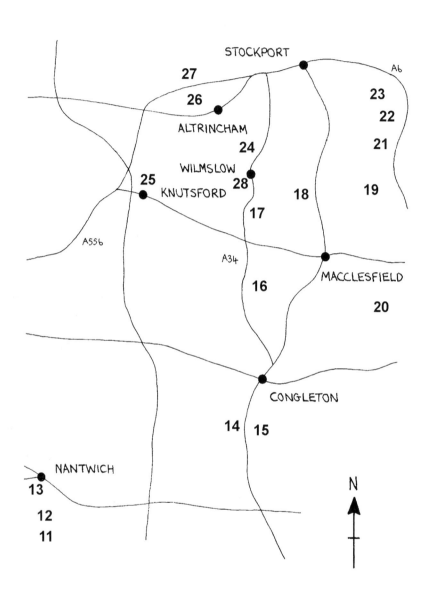

Location Map (2)

About Cheshire

Cheshire has a blend of scenery unrivalled by few other counties. In the east are the high, bleak and windswept moorlands patterned by drystone walls and riven by deep cloughs with their tumbling streams: in the west the mudflats of the Dee estuary play host to the vast wintering populations of wading birds.

The central plain noted for its languid rivers is broken by the sandstone upthrusts of Alderley Edge and the hills of Peckforton, Bickerton, Bulkeley, Frodsham and Helsby. It is dotted with Medieval, Tudor and Jacobean architectural gems built in the celebrated black and white "Magpie" style.

The green, lush pastures are grazed by countless herds of Friesians which produce the milk used in that gourmet's delight, Cheshire Cheese.

The ancient towns, Chester with its Roman remains and medieval walls, Nantwich possessed of brine springs and cathedral style parish church and Sandbach noted for its stone crosses, add an extra dimension to the countless villages with names redolent of rural England – Bunbury, Burwardsley, Tarporley, Malpas, Cholmondley, Audlem and Wybunbury.

Canals

The late eighteenth century saw the construction of several canals across Cheshire including the pioneering Bridgewater Canal in the north which gave birth to the era of Canal Mania. Others which followed were the Macclesfield, the Trent and Mersey and several shorter ones which were later amalgamated into the Shropshire Union with its branch to Llangollen, often referred to as the Llangollen Canal.

This is not the place to discuss the history of these but, even though commercial traffic no longer plies these waterways they are all used extensively by pleasure boats.

More importantly, they have bequeathed a legacy of tow-paths which, in recent years, have been repaired and upgraded for use by walkers. In this collection several stretches have been used to provide useful links between other paths in order that circular routes could be devised. In most cases, they pass through some delightful scenery, thereby adding an extra dimension to the walk.

The Walks

These routes enable the walker to explore the rich tapestry of the Cheshire countryside at leisure, often allowing him or her to discover hidden corners of great beauty which are denied to the motorist.

For those in search of challenge there are tough uphill routes, especially those walks through the moorland districts in the east of the county and those traversing the sandstone ridges. However, for the most part, they offer easy walks ideally suited for parents with young children or for those preferring gentle strolls in the evenings or on hot, lazy afternoons. Few are longer than five miles thereby allowing ample time for observation of the points of historical interest and wildlife along the way. Of course, no walk would be complete without frequent pauses to admire the scenery and the views of which there is an abundance.

The Teashops

There is no pleasanter way to end a country walk than by having a leisurely cream tea or even a cuppa in a tea shop which is also an integral part of Cheshire.

Everybody has their ideal of what a country cafe should be but, as in other walks of life, even the cafes are changing. The cosy establishment with linen tablecloths and bone china may still be found but others are of the self service variety.

Cafes do not appear to be as widespread as they once were although some new ones opened their doors whilst this book was in preparation. Sadly, others closed. It is their distribution that has dictated the locations of the walks included in this selection. One is housed in a medieval monastic refectory, another reflects the age of the Penny Farthing while a third has a truly Dickensian atmosphere. In others you can enjoy your tea in the station waiting room as the trains roll by, absorb the atmosphere of an eighteenth century cotton mill or contemplate your purchase of a Royal Worcester dinner service.

No matter which you choose you can be certain of an afternoon tea where the scones are smothered in local cream and jam followed by irresistible mouth-watering cakes, all home-baked and accompanied by a large pot of freshly brewed tea. Alternatively you may prefer a morning coffee or light lunch when you will also be assured of a warm, welcoming environment.

The opening times listed for each cafe or restaurant were correct at the time of writing and were re-checked as late as possible.

However, they may change. So, before embarking on your walk it may be as well if you check with the establishment. To facilitate this the telephone numbers have been listed. Please note that some cafes open for shorter hours during the winter months while some close completely.

PLEASE, as an act of courtesy and common sense, remove your muddy boots before entering because many of the tea rooms are luxuriously carpeted.

Tourist Information

Cheshire is rich in tourist attractions ranging from the Roman remains in the City of Chester through the collection of medieval churches to such modern developments as Jodrell Bank with its radio telescope and planetarium.

References to most of these are included in the text but there is no space in a book of this type to provide details of all of these but leaflets and booklets about all of them may be obtained from:

Tourism and Marketing Unit
Cheshire County Council,
Commerce House,
Hunter Street,
Chester CH1 2QP. Phone: Chester (01244) 603107.

Tourist Information Centres are located at:

Chester TIC
Town Hall,
Northgate Street,
Chester CH1 2HJ. Phone: Chester (01244) 402111

Congleton TIC
Town Hall,
High Street,
Congleton CW12 1BN. Phone: Congleton (01260) 271095

Ellesmere Port and Neston TIC
Council Offices,
Civic Way,
Ellesmere Port L65 0BE. Phone: 0151-356 6789

Knutsford TIC
Council Offices,
Toft Road,
Knutsford WA16 6TA. Phone: Knutsford (01565) 632611/632210

Vale Royal TIC
Wyvern House
The Drumber,
Winsford CW7 1AH. Phone: Northwich (01606) 353534.

Nantwich TIC
Church House,
The Square
Nantwich. Phone: Nantwich (01270) 610983

Macclesfield TIC
Town Hall,
Macclesfield,
SK10 1DX. Phone: Macclesfield (01625) 504114/504115

Most local libraries also contain a tourist information point stocking leaflets and other details of local tourist attractions.

Public Transport

All the walks in this book are accessible by public transport. Relevant details are provided about bus or train services at the start of each route. However, in these days of deregulation services are liable to frequent alterations. Cheshire County Council publishes a series of bus and train time-tables covering the whole county which are available, free of charge, from the Tourism and Marketing Unit at Commerce House, Hunter Street, Chester. The County Council also maintains a number of Cheshire Bus Hotlines to provide up-to-date information regarding services and changes.

They are as follows:

Warrington: (01925) 444250
Wilmslow: (01625) 534850
Crewe: (01270) 505350
Chester: (01244) 602666
Northwich: (01606) 815050

Detailed information about train times may be obtained by ringing Timetable and Fare enquiries on : 08457 48 49 50

Clothing and Equipment

Good clothing and equipment will not only increase your safety prospects but also add to your enjoyment. Obviously clothing is mainly a matter of personal choice but there are some general guidelines. Jeans, for example, are not advisable in wet, cold weather because they can be a serious hazard in combating hypothermia.

A good pair of walking boots or shoes is essential, even on lower ground where paths can be very muddy, especially after a prolonged period of wet weather. Any good stockist will offer a wide range so you can choose to suit your pocket.

Sandles and high heeled shoes are not suitable for country walking. They offer no protection against wet conditions and increase the possibility of a twisted ankle. Remember that walking boots have specially designed treads to increase their grip in slippery conditions. It is advisable to wear two pairs of walking socks so allow for this when buying your boots.

Because the British climate is so variable a cagoule and over-trousers should be carried at all times. Again go for quality when buying but avoid the heavy, rubberised variety because these will cause undue condensation. Today there is a choice of breathable fabrics such as Gore-Tex, but they are expensive.

An extra pullover is another essential because on the higher ground the temperature is always a few degrees lower than in the valley bottoms. Clothing should not to be too tightly fitting but reasonably loose and comfortable. Avoid anything which will catch on barbed wire or hedges.

In winter, when conditions may be far more severe, extra clothing should be worn. Two light pullovers are warmer than a single heavy one. Extremities should be covered because it is from these that the greatest loss of body-heat occurs. A warm woolly hat, which can be pulled down over the face and ears is a must. Gloves should be worn.

Always carry a first-aid kit in case of cuts or minor accidents. Another useful item is a pocket knife. On most of these walks you are unlikely to encounter problems but, to call for assistance, a whistle is a useful tool.

Again food is a matter of personal choice but ensure that at all times you carry some emergency rations in the form of chocolate bars which will provide energy in case of delay.

A good day sack should prove more than adequate for all the walks contained in this selection.

Walk 1. Parkgate

Route: Old Baths – Gayton – Backwood Hall – Brookhouse – Wirral Way – Old Quay – The Parade – Old Baths.

Start: The Old Baths car park, Parkgate, Wirral. Map reference 274789.

Distance: 6½ miles

Map: "Wirral & Chester/Caer", no. 266 in the O.S Explorer series.

Public Transport: Parkgate has frequent daily buses from Chester, Birkenhead, Hoylake and Meols. No Sunday service.

By Car: Parkgate is approached by either the B5134, the B5135 or the B5136 from the A540 Chester to Hoylake road. There is a small car park off Mostyn Square in the centre of the village but the Old Baths car park, just beyond the Boat House pub, usually has spare places.

The Tea Shop

The Parkgate Coffee Shop on the Parade not only offers a fine view out over the Dee Estuary but also provides everything from a cup of tea to substantial snacks. It has a mouth-watering selection of home-made cakes and some of the best cream scones you are likely to see in Cheshire. Housed in one of the old seafront houses, it comes complete with wooden beams and photos of Parkgate in bygone days.

Opening Hours: Tuesday to Friday, 9.15am to 5pm; Saturday and Sunday, 10am to 5pm. Closed Mondays. Phone: 0151 336 4414.

Parkgate

When the River Dee silted up and large ships were no longer able to reach Chester, Parkgate became the chief port of embarkation for Ireland. At high tide it was not unknown for the Parade to be flooded. During the nineteenth century it also developed as a fashionable resort.

Today it is no longer a port, separated from the narrow channel of the river by enormous grass and reed covered marshes which are the haunt of thousands of wading birds in winter. The front is lined with attractive houses and cottages and it is renowned for the shellfish on sale in some of the fish shops.

The large black and white house, now Mostyn House School, was once a hotel where Handel stayed while waiting for a packet boat to Dublin for the first performance of his "Messiah".

Mostyn House, Parkgate

Lady Hamilton was born near Parkgate so, according to local tradition, Admiral Nelson may have sailed into Parkgate for a romantic tryst.

The Route

Leave the Old Baths car park to proceed through the picnic area in a northerly direction with the silted-up River Dee on your left. The course of the river is an apparently endless mass of grass and other vegetation. Do not be tempted to walk on this because it is full of quicksand and riven by numerous water courses.

On your right is hawthorn, ragwort and an abundance of guelder rose beyond which is a golf course. This, in turn, gives way to a succession of open fields. Ignore a sign on your right to the Wirral Way and, after a little over a mile and by a white house, the path curves round to the right before descending a flight of six steps onto the end of a minor road.

Walk along this away from the River Dee, passing "Gayton Cottage" on your left, and proceeding for a quarter of a mile until it climbs slightly to cross a railway bridge. About 50 metres beyond this turn right through a waymarked gap and double back to reach the bed of a former railway track. This is the Wirral Way. Turn left.

This 12-mile walking trail follows the line of the axed railway from

Hooton in Cheshire to West Kirby in Merseyside. Guide books are available from Tourist Information Centres in the area.

After negotiating the gap in a wooden barrier, the Wirral Way dips into a shallow hollow and climbs again to cross a wide track linking two sections of the golf course. 100 metres beyond this intersection, and with wooden five-barred gates flanking both sides of the track, turn left through a waymarked wooden kissing gate.

Follow the path over the links, staying between the two lines of thin blue poles. Climb gradually through a line of trees and to the left of a solitary sandstone gatepost before ascending a flight of three steps on the boundary of the golf course.

At the top turn right to follow a distinct path through a belt of trees but, after 100 metres, swing to the right over a planked footbridge and then turn sharp left to proceed along the very edge of the golf course.

There is a hedge and fence on your left matched, on your right, by a fine perspective out over the Dee Estuary to the Welsh coast with the Clywydian hills forming the backdrop. The grass path makes for excellent walking.

Negotiate a waymarked ladder stile before following the obvious path over the centre of a field to reach a footbridge with a stile at either end. Climb to the left of a fence for 50 metres to a small white wooden gate.

Through that continue for a further 50 metres along a wide track to a black and white wooden five-barred gate and then maintain direction to the left of the red sandstone wall which forms the boundary of Backwood Hall, the farm on your right. Remain with this track, which develops into a hedged lane, until it meets Boathouse Lane by a footpath finger post.

Cross directly into Wood Lane, remaining with it beyond the end of Brook Lane which comes in from Brook House on your left. About 100 metres beyond, turn right through waymarked wooden posts onto a fenced path. A few metres before a bridge which spans the path, veer right up another path which leads onto the Wirral Way after 10 metres.

Turn left over the bridge. Where the Wirral Way appears to reach a dead-end, turn left through a wooden barrier and then turn right to arrive at a five-barred gate after 100 metres. This provides an exit onto Station Road.

Turn right for a few metres. Pass the Parkgate village sign and the Conservation Area sign with its full-rigged sailing ship, and then make a left turn by the Wirral Country Park sign to re-join the Wirral Way.

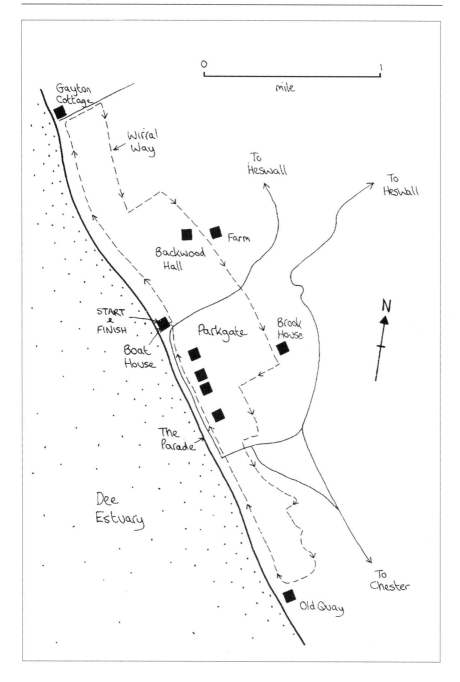

At the top of the approach to the former Parkgate Railway Station, where the surfaced road bends sharply to the left towards the toilet block, stay forward through a wooden barrier. Initially there are tennis courts on your right before the route pursues its course between birch and other trees, passes under an arched bridge and through another wooden barrier before reaching an intersection.

Ignore the path to the left signed to Neston. Instead make a right turn to pass a fairly inconspicuous sign which reads, "To Old Quay Lane".

The well-defined path traverses open country between a fence on the left and a hedgerow on the right until it meets Old Quay Lane. Turn left along this narrow surfaced road leading to the Sewage Treatment Works owned by Welsh Water PLC. However, do not proceed as far as the plant.

Where the road bends acutely to the right, maintain your direction through an old metal kissing gate adjacent to a (currently) decrepit metal five-barred gate. Through this, and ignoring the path leading directly ahead, fork right through a hedge gap and then veer left over the open field following another well-trodden path until it forms a T-junction in mid field with a wider grass track. Turn right along this, cross a footbridge and continue across the next field to the right of a hedge before negotiating a second metal kissing gate.

Beyond, maintain direction until reaching a small flight of stone steps. There, turn right along the path which charts a course through the substantial stone remnants of the old quay.

Add a little romance to your excursion by pausing a while to imagine sailing ships from all four corners of the globe once berthing at this point to discharge and load their cargoes. Then it would have been a bustling, thriving spot livened by the creaking of ships' timbers and the rumble of cart wheels. Today it is a scene of peace and tranquillity. The remains are surrounded by green fields and, where the river once flowed there is a sea of reeds and grass where the flocks of goldfinch and other birds roost.

Through the ruins follow the path across an area of scrub. Over the first stile, keep to the narrow path which clings close to the fence until, after half a mile and facing a bungalow, it swings round to the right to emerge into a modern housing estate by Old Quay Close.

Turn left along Manorial Road, ignoring the fact that it is signed as a cul-de-sac. At the far end continue along the path signed, "To The Parade". After 100 metres this widens into an unadopted road.

By a large black and white house turn right to a T-junction. Turn left along Hunter's Close and, with the cricket ground on your right, advance to re-join Station Road opposite a row of old fishermen's cottages. Turn left for 100 metres before turning right along the Parade.

This is the time to treat yourself to a cream tea in the Parkgate Coffee Shop, to admire the architecture, to sample the seafood in the fish shops and to absorb the view.

At the far end, where the road bends to the right, stay forward and, keeping the Boat House pub on your left, walk the final 200 metres to your starting point.

Walk 2. Willaston

Route: Hadlow Lane car park – Willaston Grange – Chester High Road – Foxes Farm – Hallwood Farm – Oak Farm – Hadlow Lane.

Start: Wirral Way car park, Hadlow Lane, Willaston, Wirral. Map reference 331773

Distance: 4½ miles.

Map: "Wirral & Chester/Caer", no. 266 in the O.S. Explorer series.

Public Transport: Willaston village is less than a quarter of a mile from the starting point. It is served by daily buses from Chester, Parkgate, West Kirby, Meols and Heswall. There are daily buses (not Sundays) from Ellesmere Port. Some buses connect at Hooton with trains from Chester, Birkenhead and Liverpool.

By Car: The start is off Hadlow Lane, Willaston, from where it is signed as Wirral Country Park. Both the village and car park are signed from the A540 at map reference 326763. The Country Park is also signed from the centre of Willaston village which stands on the B5133.

The Tea Shop

The Gordale Garden Centre has a large, new restaurant with a floral ambience. It offers a wide-ranging menu including light lunches, baked potatoes with a variety of fillings, sandwiches, cheese and onion pasties, Cornish pasties, sausage rolls, soup of the day with rolls and an amazing variety of gateaux and cakes including scones, Victoria Sponge and Chocolate Fudge Cake.

Opening Hours: Daily 9.15am to 6.00pm all year (extended to 8.00pm on Thursdays except for January and February), phone: 0151 336 8152.

Willaston

Willaston is an attractive village in the middle of the Wirral Peninsula with a half timbered inn dating from the reign of Charles I and small cottages clustered around a green. Willaston Hall is even older and is renowned for its splendid Elizabethan front. The church which is built in the Gothic style dates from the nineteenth century and is distinguished by its very steep roof and its bellcot.

The station at Hadlow Road

The Route

After having had a look around the restored station of Hadlow Road, complete with its 1950s atmosphere, proceed to the far end of the car park, pass through the barrier and continue for approximately 50 metres to a wooden finger post.

The single arm indicates a path to Wallcroft which heads off to the left. Ignore this, choosing rather to make a right turn across the horse riders' track to negotiate a facing stile before traversing the first field while keeping close to a large barn and silo tower on your right.

Over the next stile, cross a lane to a facing waymarked stile and continue in the same direction to the left of a fence and hedge. On the far side of this field cross the planked footbridge to a footpath sign and stile which provides an exit onto New Hey Lane, a minor road.

Turn right for about 150 metres to another footpath sign. By this make a left turn over a footbridge, negotiate a waymarked stile and proceed along the boundary of a field passing Willaston Grange with its tennis courts to your right.

Beyond the next stile maintain direction over a cultivated field and remain to the left of a cottage before arriving at a rough track. Cross this directly to a very low waymarker post and continue through a belt of trees while remaining to the immediate left of a high brick wall.

On meeting another track, after 100 metres cross to a waymarked wooden stile before continuing along the right-hand side of a long, narrow paddock where horses graze. Beyond the next stile, stay forward over another cultivated field whilst aiming for a hedge corner where, eventually, you will find a stile. Over this, turn left through ninety degrees and, staying close to the hedge on your right and circling round a large pond, continue until another stile permits an exit onto the A540, known at this point as "The Chester High Road".

Turn left and, walking along the pavement, reach the Gordale Garden Centre for a welcome break. Suitably refreshed continue along the A540, passing in turn the Water Gardens and the Burton Garden Centre. Some 10 metres before a sign indicating a side road to Ness Gardens and Burton look for a footpath finger post on your left. By this, turn left through a metal kissing gate and, clinging to the field boundary, advance along the whole length of the field, keeping a wary eye open for the bull which, according to the notice, is present in the field.

Over the stile in the far corner stay to the left of a hedge but, over the next stile, veer right towards an obvious gateway with a large circular galvanised metal cattle trough some three metres to its left. Proceed through the gate to enter a lane which leads beyond Foxes Farm and an equestrian tack shop before passing to the left of Hallwood Farm to meet a minor road on a right-angled bend.

Do not go quite as far as the road. Instead, turn left along the driveway to Oak Farm which, according to the notices, has a fine herd of Friesian cattle. After almost half a mile along this surfaced lane keep to the left of Oak Farm and maintain direction through the farm yard. After a second metal gate the track becomes an ordinary country lane.

Pass to the right of a third gate, where a smaller one for pedestrian access is missing. Keep forward for a further 20 metres to another minor road, also on a sharp bend. Turn left along this road which, just beyond "July Cottage", provides the only climb of the walk as it rises for 100 metres to pass over a redbrick bridge spanning a disused railway line.

A hundred metres beyond the bridge, and at the bottom of the slope and by a footpath sign, make an acute turn to the left. Pass through the wooden barrier after 100 metres and turn right along the Wirral Way. Now well-established, this popular walking route is acquiring a mature vegetation which includes several varieties of tree and such plants as guelder rose, giant hogweed, bramble and rosebay willowherb.

In spring and early summer the trees resound to the calls of wrens, blackbirds, thrushes, titmice and the ubiquitous magpie with its cousin, the jay. Follow the track, eschewing any side paths, until reaching your starting point at Hadlow Road station.

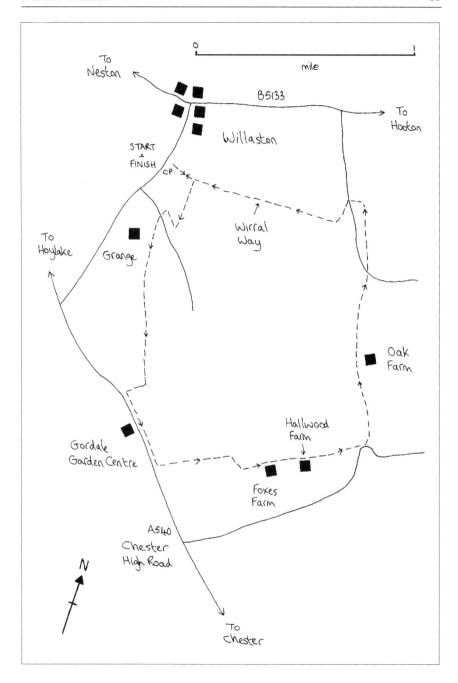

Walk 3. Chester

Route: Northgate car park – Upper Northgate – City Walls – Newgate – Souter's Lane – The Groves – Old Dee Bridge – Bridge Street – The Cross – Eastgate – St Werburgh Street – Abbey Gate – Northgate – Northgate car park.

Start: Northgate long stay car park, off Northgate Avenue. Map reference 403671.

Distance: 3½ miles.

Maps: 1. "Wirral & Chester/Caer", no. 266 in the O.S. Explorer series; 2. Town street plan from the Tourist Information Centre.

Public Transport: Chester is served by daily buses from London, Manchester, Liverpool, Birkenhead, Nantwich, Shrewsbury, Whitchurch, Northwich, Wrexham and Stoke-on-Trent and other towns as well as numerous local services. The bus station is off Northgate, close to the starting point of the walk. There are trains from London, Manchester, Liverpool, North Wales, Shrewsbury, Whitchurch, Liverpool, Birkenhead, Northwich and Crewe.

By Car: Chester is at the focal point of several major roads including the M53/56 from Birkenhead and Manchester, the A41 from the Wirral and Whitchurch, the A5104 from Mold, the A483 from Wrexham, the A61 from Nantwich, the A54 from Middlewich and Congleton and the A556 from Manchester. Apart from the Northgate long stay car park there are several others in and around the city but some are short stay only.

The Tea Shop

There are several excellent tea shops and cafes in the city area but the most unusual is the Refectory Tea Shop. Reached through the Cathedral and the Cloisters this spacious and atmospheric tea room is housed in the thirteenth century Refectory, the dining room used by the monks of this Benedictine Abbey before Henry VIII's Reformation led to it being converted into the present Cathedral of St Werburgh to serve the newly created Diocese of Chester. It must be the only tea shop in Britain that boasts a genuine pulpit. It was from this that one of the monks would read passages from the Bible while his brethren ate their meals in silence.

A huge tapestry on the west wall shows St Paul confronting the sorcerer Elymas on Cyprus. Woven at Mortlake during the seventeenth century it is based on a drawing by Raphael. The arms of the powerful Earls of Chester are featured in a heraldic display on the north wall.

In sharp contrast to the frugal fare of the medieval diners the Refectory today offers a menu that is positively sinful. For the morning walker there is an "Early Breakfast" which is designed to satisfy any trencherman while lunches include items such as steak and mushroom pie and lasagne, not to mention the daily specials.

For the afternoon walker there is a range of afternoon teas all of which include scones with an abundance of cream, home-made gateaux and a choice of speciality teas. Any medieval monastic ghosts hovering about the place must assume that every day is Christmas.

Opening hours: 1st April to 31st October, 9.30 a.m. to 4.45p.m; 1st November to 31st March, 10.00 a.m. to 4.15p.m; Daily except Sundays. Phone: 01244 313156

Chester

It can truly be said that the history of Chester is the history of England in miniature. Roman garrison, site of a powerful medieval abbey transformed into a cathedral at the Reformation, bustling port during the Middle Ages that provided the gateway to Ireland, Marcher town fortified against the marauding Welsh, site of the last major conflict of the Civil War, an important coaching and later railway centre and county town, Chester has always been a vibrant, thriving city.

Today the visitor may enjoy the legacy of this rich tapestry which history has bequeathed to Chester. The Roman ruins, the Cathedral, the plethora of splendid black and white Tudor buildings, the riverside and the Rows – Europe's first undercover shopping mall – all combine to give the city a unique charm.

The Route

From the car park entrance turn left along Northgate Avenue and, at the first junction, turn left again into Victoria Avenue to pass Abbey Gate School on your right.

Keeping the Northgate Arena on your left, follow the pavement round to the left until reaching a pedestrian subway. Descend the steps, turn right at the bottom and, at the far end of the tunnel, turn right up another flight of steps. On emerging at street level stay forward to a large traffic island with fountains in the centre.

Here turn left into Upper Northgate Street soon passing the Bluecoat School on your right and crossing over the Shropshire Union Canal by a

Chester Cathedral

high bridge. A short distance to your right is the narrow Bridge of Sighs once used by condemned felons on their way to the Chapel of Little St John shortly before execution.

Immediately afterwards go under the sandstone arch of Northgate and turn sharp left up the steps. At the top make a right turn to follow the City Walls which, although repaired and rebuilt several times, have protected Chester since Roman times.

The shops on your right soon give way to Abbey Green followed by the Dean's Garden and a cricket field. The sound of leather on willow has replaced the clash of steel created by soldiers in training because the garrison's barracks occupied this site two thousand years ago. In summer pleasure craft ply the canal which is a long way down below on your left. Despite its proximity to the city centre it is also graced by mallard, coot and moorhen.

By the first corner stands King Charles' Tower, a reconstructed medieval building, now housing a souvenir shop and museum but from which Charles I watched his troops being defeated at the Battle of Rowton Moor in 1645. From the tower continue along the walls but now in a southerly direction with the Cathedral a short distance to the right. Climb the short flight of steps leading up to the celebrated Clock Tower which spans Eastgate. Built in 1897 to commemorate Queen Victoria's

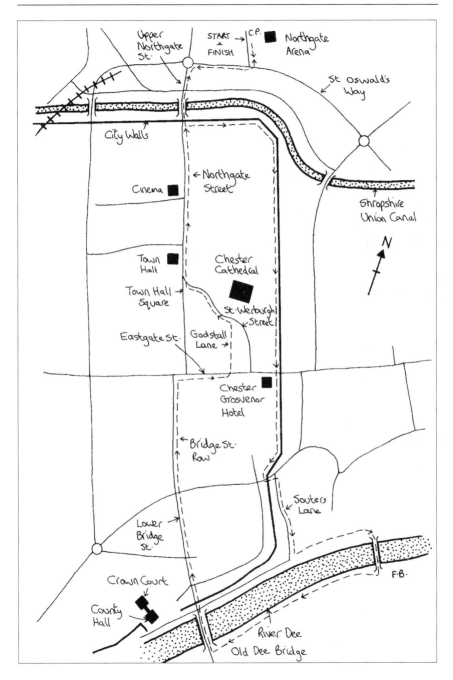

Diamond Jubilee, this affords a bird's eye view along Eastgate with its collection of black and white buildings, many dating back to Tudor and even medieval times.

Continue along the walls to Newgate which crosses over St John Street with the Roman Amphitheatre down below on your left. Cross the bridge before descending the steps into Park Street. At the bottom turn right into Little St John Street and, after 10 metres, make another right turn for a visit to the Roman Gardens with their collection of imperial stone columns and hypercaust.

Leave the gardens by the same entrance and make a right turn along Little StJohn Street. After ten metres turn right into Souter's Lane which is signed to the River Dee and provides a passageway to The Groves.

By the landing stage used by the pleasure cruisers, turn left along the Groves with its large collection of seats and bandstand.

On approaching the conspicuous white metal suspension bridge, veer left a few metres before it to make a sharp turn to the right onto the bridge itself.

This footbridge, one of the famous landmarks of the Chester waterfront, was built in 1923 to link the city with the suburb of Handbridge.

At the far end turn right, descend a flight of steps and turn left along the riverside path. With the Dee graced by its swans on your right, pass the restored mill water wheel and an enormous weir to reach the Old Dee Bridge.

This occupies the site of a Roman bridge and was worthy of a mention in that national inventory, the Domesday Book, in 1086. The original structure, presumably of wood, was replaced by stone in 1387 and for hundreds of years remained the only bridge spanning the Dee at Chester. It was widened by the Victorians but retained its medieval appearance and today's single line traffic is regulated by lights.

Climb the short flight of steps opposite the Roman shrine to Minerva to exit onto Handbridge. Turn right over the Old Dee Bridge and keeping the Castle, now rebuilt as an assize court on your left, maintain your direction into Lower Bridge Street.

In the course of climbing this historic street you will pass "The Bear and Billet", built in 1664, "Ye Olde King's Head" from 1662 and Gamul House where a brick facade conceals a Jacobean Hall. This was the home of Sir Francis Gamul who was Mayor of Chester in 1635 and it was here, in September, 1645, that Charles I lodged on the eve of the Battle of Rowton Moor.

Further along you will also pass the early eighteenth-century

Oddfellows Hall and the Toy Museum which houses a collection of Victorian dolls, teddy bears and 1920s pedal cars alongside train sets and Dinky cars. It is a veritable Aladdin's Cave for young children and those adults possessed of a strong sense of nostalgia.

At the junction of Bridge Street with Grosvenor Street and Pepper Street stands the Chester Heritage Centre housed in the former St Michael's Church. It relates the story of the city over the last 2,000 years through displays and audio-visual presentations.

Immediately on your left, and on the opposite corner to the Heritage Centre, is "The Falcon", a half-timbered seventeenth century building formerly used as a Temperance Room. Restored and ironically converted into a pub in 1982, it has won one of the highest conservation accolades, a Europa Nostra Award for the work carried out.

From this interesting cross roads continue forwards into Bridge Street, passing even more examples of black and white magpie architecture and meeting the first of the celebrated Rows.

Furious debates still persist over the reasons behind these covered shopping arcades but the stone undercrofts appear to have been built in the late thirteenth century, shortly after the Great Fire of 1278 which destroyed most of the city.

Stay with Bridge Street as far as The Cross. This, the traditional centre of Chester, stands at the junction of the four main streets, Eastgate, Northgate, Bridge Street and Watergate. As its name implies, Watergate led down to the harbour in the years when Chester was a thriving port.

The Cross was carved from local sandstone in the fifteenth century and has been restored following damage during the Civil War. It is now used as the principal station for the Town Crier at midday and at three o'clock every afternoon from Tuesday to Saturday between Easter and the end of September. By The Cross turn right along Eastgate and then turn left into the very narrow Godstall Lane, staying with it until emerging into St Werburgh Street opposite the Cathedral entrance.

Turn left along St Werburgh Street following it round until it forms a junction with Northgate opposite the imposing Town Hall. Turn right to retrace your steps to the starting point.

Walk 4. Frodsham

Route: Beacon Hill – Shepherd's Houses – Dober's Lane – Riley Bank – Snidley Moor – Woodhouse Hill – Dunsdale Hollow – Jacob's Ladder – Beacon Hill.

Start: Beacon Hill car park, Frodsham. Map reference 518766.

Distance: 4 / miles.

Map: "Northwich & Delamere Forest", no. 267 in the O.S. Explorer series.

Public Transport: Frodsham is served by frequent daily (including Sundays) buses from Chester, Runcorn, Widnes, and Warrington. Buses from Northwich Mondays to Saturdays. Frodsham has frequent daily (including Sundays) trains from Chester, Manchester Piccadilly, Liverpool, Warrington and Runcorn.

By Car: Frodsham is located on the A56, Chester to Warrington road. It is also signed from Junction 12 of the M56 Motorway. There are several car parks in the town centre, in addition to the starting point at Beacon Hill. Parking may be difficult on Thursday which is market day.

The Tea Shop

The Cottage Tea Shop, standing on the north side of Main Street, Frodsham, lives up to its name. The owners have created a warm, intimate atmosphere with lace-covered circular tables, spindle-backed chairs, a genuine beamed ceiling typical of the building's antiquity, and small wall niches decorated with fancy tea pots and copper kettles.

There is a wide range of speciality teas, brewed in large pots, and a selection of coffees and other beverages. Light meals and snacks are available while you can choose between an afternoon tea and a Cream Tea with a variety of home-made cakes rarely found elsewhere. These include carrot cake, chocolate cake, lemon meringue pie which dissolves in the mouth, Victoria sponge and Genoa cake.

Opening hours: All year. Mondays to Fridays, 10.00 a.m. to 4.30 p.m; Saturdays, 10.00 a.m. to 4.00 p.m; Closed on Sundays; Phone: 01928 733673

Frodsham

The presence of several hill forts behind the town suggests that the settlements in this area were of ancient origin. Frodsham also stands on the route of the Roman road from Chester to Wilderspool, near Warrington.

The Norman Earls of Chester constructed a fort in the town which survived until the seventeenth century. Its site is now occupied by Castle Park. Frodsham's importance during the coaching era is recalled by such inns as the "Bear's Paw", obviously the scene of bear baiting, and the Queen's Hotel. The parish church is of Norman origin.

The Route

To avoid a steep climb of more than a mile through the suburban streets of Frodsham, it is suggested that you start from Beacon Hill, the northern terminus of the Sandstone Trail. To reach it from Main Street, Frodsham, turn into Church Street, proceeding uphill before making a right turn into Church Road, which is signed to the parish church.

Opposite the church turn left into Bellemonte Road and follow this around its tortuous course until reaching Beacon Hill car park located immediately beneath the massive radio towers.

From Beacon Hill car park make a left turn along Simoons Lane, soon passing Overhill Cottage on your left. Ignore a three-armed finger post, continuing until approximately 50 metres beyond the entrance to Frodsham Golf Club on your right.

By the footpath sign go right over the stile to keep close company with the boundary fence of the golf club which is on the right. Beyond the next stile the path continues between a hedge and a fence as it climbs gradually to provide a view of the Welsh Hills in the far distance ahead.

Ignore a stile and signed path running off to the left, staying forward to rendezvous with the lane which leads to Mickledale Farm. Cross to the facing stile before veering gradually left with the distinct path as it crosses a field to a stile by a footpath sign.

This provides an exit onto Manley Road. Turn right for 100 metres but, by Shepherd's Houses, turn left into Dober's Lane, a sandy track. Climb gradually to the left of Harrol Edge with its underground reservoir until meeting a minor road on a sharp bend.

Ignore this road. Instead turn sharp right into an unsigned lane which runs just below the reservoir. Eventually it loses height to another minor road. Turn right for a short climb to a Y-junction.

Fork right for the descent of Riley's Bank, with Riley Bank Mews on your left, to reach the B5393. Cross the T-junction to a facing ladder stile and descend the field gradually while staying close to the fence on your right. Towards the far end of this field the path suddenly cork-screws steeply down a bank to a ladder stile in a hollow.

Over the stile remain with the distinct path, curving to the right as directed by the yellow waymarker, to lose even more height through a wooded clough until reaching two separate waymarker posts in the bottom of a valley which has an atmosphere of utter remoteness.

Turn left along the broad track running along the valley floor. Negotiate a stile adjacent to a five-barred metal gate and stay forward, the slope on your right being carpeted with bracken which creates an ideal habitat for the wrens and robins to be observed along this stretch of the route.

On reaching a Y-junction fork left, remaining on the lower ground just to the right of a wire fence and parallel with some overhead wires.

Arriving at another stile alongside a metal five-barred gate, navigate carefully. Over the stile ignore a steep track going off at right angles. Instead, advance about six metres before turning right through another five-barred gate, as indicated by a faded waymark, to walk a wide lane hedged on your left and fenced on your right.

This track runs parallel with The Ridgeway, a short distance away on the crest of the slope to your left. As the name suggests, this is an ancient route but, sadly for today's walker, it is a surfaced road.

The Cottage Tea Shop

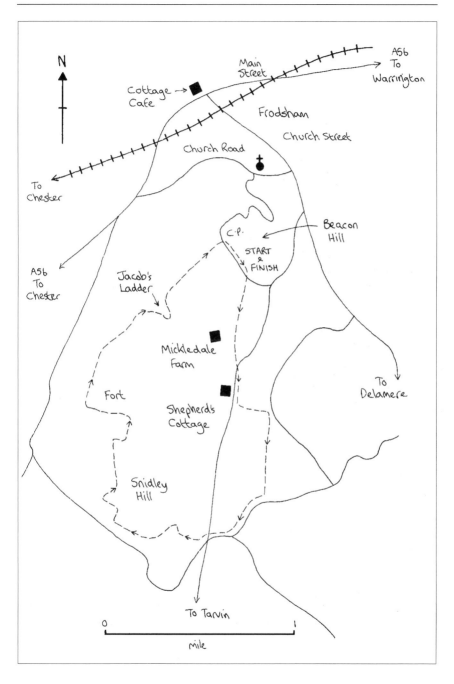

After a mere 50 metres the track passes through a gateway. On the far side turn sharply to the left and clinging closely to the hedge, follow a narrower path along the bottom of a sloping field until a stile provides access to a lane.

Turn right along this, a part of the Sandstone Trail. It climbs gradually for more than a mile through the woodlands of Snidley Moor, large swathes of which have recently been re-planted by the owners, the Woodland Trust.

It is refreshing to see a discreet notice, informing members of the public that they are free to wander through the trees flanking both sides and, to prove that this is no empty invitation, several paths rise up the steep slopes.

The Sandstone Trail continues its meandering upwards course through the woods guided by frequent waymarks. Large blocks of red sandstone are often embedded in the surface.

On arriving at a Y-junction close to the summit of Snidley Moor, fork left for 20 metres to a T-junction. Turn left as the track continues rising, this time up the slopes of Woodhouse Hill.

A brief opening in the woodland on your right permits a view of Beacon Hill but soon the route swings round to the right and re-enters more woodland to cross the site of Woodhouse Hill Fort, constructed during the Iron Age by some of Cheshire's earliest inhabitants.

The track emerges from the woods onto the summit of a sheer, high cliff where one of the finest views in Cheshire literally takes your breath away. You gaze out over the M56 Motorway to the vast expanse of Frodsham Marshes, one of the most significant ornithological sites in Britain. Beyond, the Mersey forms an enormous sweep into its estuary as it separates Lancashire from the Wirral and approaches Liverpool with the distinctive towers of its twin cathedrals dominating the distant skyline.

Having absorbed the vista, descend steeply for 50 metres to a waymarker post and turn right and walk along the cliff edge. If you have children do not let them run freely at this point.

Soon, the path meets and runs just to the left of the fence of Frodsham Golf Course. Although there is no waymarker at this point, corner right, with the fence. A short distance beyond, the path loses height dramatically as it descends Abraham's Leap into Dunsdale Hollow where high sandstone cliffs on the right are pitted with caves resulting from erosion by wind, rain and frost. Walkers interested in etymology will be delighted to learn that "Dunsdale Hollow" interprets as "Valley of Dung".

By the waymarker post at the foot of Abraham's Leap turn left. Almost immediately there is a stile on the right which is waymarked, but not with the Sandstone Trail logo. Do not be tempted by it. Prefer, instead, the main path which continues, still downhill, to the waymarker post at the foot of Jacob's Ladder, a staircase path carved out of the rock face.

Today this dangerous exit from Dunsdale Hollow is avoided. By the waymarker post turn right for some 50 metres before turning left for a steep ascent of a flight of steps with a convenient handrail on which someone has carved the words, "Not So Far Now".

From the top of these steps the path levels as it runs along the cliff to a stile providing access to the golf course. Taking your line of direction from a waymarker and aiming to the right of a solitary gorse bush, cross the links to a narrow hedged corridor and the final stile. Continue a further few metres to Simoons Lane and make a right turn to your starting point. When ready, drive into the centre of Frodsham for that well-earned afternoon tea at the Cottage Cafe on Main Street

Walk 5. Delamere Forest

Route: Delamere Station – Eddisbury Hill – Roman Road – King's Chair – Eddisbury Lodge – Visitor Centre – Delamere Station.

Start: Delamere railway station. Map reference 556703

Distance: 4 miles

Map: "Northwich & Delamere Forest", no. 267 in the O.S. Explorer series.

Public Transport: Delamere railway station is served by frequent daily (including Sunday) trains from Chester, Stockport, Northwich and Manchester.

By Car: Delamere railway station is off the B5152 road from the A556 at Abbey Arms to Frodsham. There is a large car park on the picnic site.

The Tea Shop

The Station House Cafe is situated in the former station house at Delamere railway station and is, not surprisingly, decorated with railway memorabilia. Because the station is still operational you can enjoy your repast as the trains come to a halt on their way to Chester or Manchester

Its scones, with lavish helpings of cream and accompanied by generous servings of tea, are a delight. So, too, are the afternoon teas. For anyone who can take more there is a wide range of home-made cakes and fruit pies which makes choice somewhat difficult. If you are not a cholesterol seeker, the Station House Cafe also serves a menu of light meals.

Opening hours: Daily, 10.00 a.m. to 5.00 p.m; Phone: 01606 889825

Delamere Forest

When the Normans arrived in this part of Cheshire the great Forest of Mara and Mondrum, "The Forest of the Meres", covered the land between the Mersey and Nantwich. It was established as a Royal Hunting Forest and remained in use as such until the reign of Charles I.

During that period all the remaining deer were culled and, in later centuries, the great oaks were used for the building of warships. During the mid nineteenth century it was replanted but the seed used proved to be of poor quality.

After the First World War it was taken over by the Forestry Commission and coniferous species planted to maximise timber production. These included Scots and Corsican Pines, Larch and Western Hemlock.

In more recent years, in accordance with changing policy, it has been developed as a recreational amenity which has resulted in the planting of more broadleaved trees, and the provision of car parks, picnic areas, a Visitor Centre and an educational service.

The forest itself now covers 785 hectares and provides a habitat for numerous birds, including several birds of prey, insects on the meres and such mammals as fox and badger.

The Forest Visitor Centre is open: Mondays to Fridays: 10.30 a.m. to 12.30 p.m. and 13.00 p.m. to 4.15p.m; Saturdays and Sundays: 10.30 a.m. to 4.45p.m.

Eddisbury Hill

This is the site of the most complex hill fort in Cheshire. Constructed by an Iron Age community, its seven acres were surrounded and defended by a wooden palisade. Demolished by the Romans, it was briefly restored to life by Queen Ethelfleda, daughter of King Alfred, during the Saxon period of our history.

The Route

Exit the car park and picnic site by passing to the right of the Station House Cafe and proceeding along the station approach until meeting the B5152, Station Road.

Turn right and, using the pavement, walk in the direction of the A556, initially passing a golf course on your left. Soon this gives way to a panorama of open country while on your right is a succession of bungalows.

After almost a mile turn right into Eddisbury Hill for a steep climb. As soon as the houses are left behind the extensive panorama reveals the vastness of the Cheshire Plain and the Mersey Valley. On a clear day the West Pennine Moors north of Bolton are visible.

On approaching the summit of Eddisbury Hill the land is decorated by gorse and the trees house a noisy rookery. In time the going levels and you pass a white house on the right which carries the date of 1911 along with the royal coat of arms and the initials "GR".

A short distance beyond, Eddisbury Hill forms a junction with Stoney Lane. Maintain direction to a stile adjacent to a five-barred gate and a footpath sign.

Take the wide, sandy track which, according to the map, follows the route of a Roman road as it keeps along the edge of the field. Beyond the fence on your immediate right is a gathering of TV masts on the summit

Delamere Forest

of Pale Heights. Following a very gradual loss of altitude there is an at-tractive valley running off to the right but this is not on our route.

Instead, negotiate a facing stile alongside a five-barred gate before continuing to the left of a row of Scots Pines. This is followed by another gentle climb to a stile in the right-hand corner of a field. Over that, the path keeps to the left of some hawthorns and to the right of a barbed wire fence while, only a short distance below to your left, traffic roars along the A556, the Manchester to Chester road.

Following another stile maintain direction through a small planta-tion for 100 metres to a footpath finger post by a T-junction. Turn right along the Sandstone Trail so that you are walking in a northerly direc-tion.

The rise on your right is Hangingstone Hill while to your left, but no longer visible, is a quarry known as King's Chair from where stone was quarried for the construction of Vale Royal Abbey.

The good, clear path enters Nettleford Wood for a delightful slightly rising stretch to a three-armed footpath post. Ignore the path heading left and signed to Yeld Lane, opting rather to stay forward with the path signed to Barnsbridge Gates.

Negotiate a stile by a five-barred gate which provides access onto a

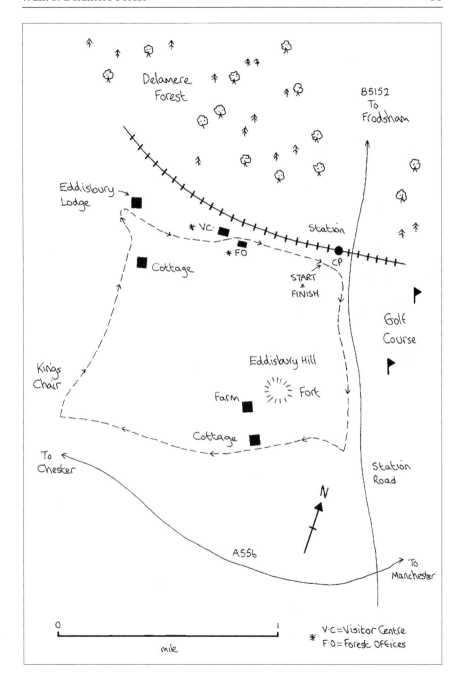

Delamere Forest

B5152
To
Frodsham

Eddisbury Lodge

* VC

* FO

Station

CP

Cottage

START
&
FINISH

Golf
Course

Eddisbury Hill

Kings
Chair

Farm   Fort

Cottage

To
Chester

Station
Road

N

A556

To
Manchester

0   1

mile

V·C = Visitor Centre
* F·O = Forest Offices

grassy path which descends gradually through an avenue of trees with distant views of Ellesmere Port and Stanlow.

As you keep "Eddisbury Lodge Cottage" on your right, the rate of descent quickens to an intersection in front of "Eddisbury Lodge". Following the sign to Delamere Station, turn right along a broad track which clings to a well-maintained holly hedge on the left as it wends its way along level ground before passing to the right of the Forestry Enterprise Visitor Centre and to the left of the Forestry Office.

On reaching a railway bridge on the left stay forward but, after a further 100 metres, turn left through a small metal gate, descend the steps and then turn right to walk through the picnic area to the car park from where you started and the Station House Cafe.

Walk 6. Blakemere

Route: Blakemere – Sandiway – Cockpit Lane – Daleford Manor – Newchurch Common – Whitegate Way – Kennel Bridge – Nunsmere – Blakemere.

Start: Blakemere Craft Centre on the A556. Map reference 598703.

Distance: 5 miles.

Map: "Northwich & Delamere Forest", no. 267 in the O.S. Explorer series.

Public Transport: There are frequent daily (including Sunday) buses to Sandiway from Northwich and Chester. There are buses from Altrincham on Sundays.

By Car: The Blakemere Craft Centre is by the A556, between the village of Sandiway and the junction of the A49 Warrington to Whitchurch road. Large car park and no admission charge.

The Tea Shop

Housed in one of the converted stable blocks, this light and airy coffee shop and restaurant is furnished with pine tables covered with linen tablecloths and matched by spindle-backed chairs. The plain white walls, with a small amount of exposed brickwork, are adorned with sprays of dried flowers. The spacious windows, with their floral curtains, offer panoramic views out over the surrounding countryside.

For the thirsty there is a wide selection of coffees, herbal and speciality teas along with soft drinks. If cream is your weakness close your eyes as you wander past the cake selection otherwise you are certain to yield to temptation. The scones, home baked, arrive under a mountain of cream and jam.

In addition there is a range of more substantial fare ranging from sandwiches, through bacon barm cakes to a choice of cooked dishes represented by quiches and lasagne. For the more health conscious there is a range of salads.

Opening Hours: All year. Tuesday to Friday: 10.00 a.m. to 5.00 p.m; Saturday and Sunday: 10.00 a.m. to 5.30 p.m; Mondays: Closed; Phone: 01606 889191 or 01606 883261

Blakemere

This craft centre, is housed around the cobbled courtyard of a former

The coffee shop, Blakemere Craft Centre

racing stable, one of the many in this area of central Cheshire. The red-brick Edwardian buildings have been carefully and tastefully restored to accommodate a wide variety of crafts people selling their products. Embroidery, hand-knitted goods, furniture, dried flowers, hand-made chocolates, American crafts, pottery and numerous other goods are on sale.

The Route

Leaving the car park strike out diagonally across the open space to the corner of the main building and, staying to the left of this, take the short footpath leading to the A556, Chester Road. Exercising caution, cross to the far side and turn right to walk eastwards along the pavement for approximately half a mile passing through a part of Sandiway village.

Beyond the traffic lights, and by the far corner of the wooden boundary fence of Sandiway Grange, now a residential home for the elderly, turn right into Cockpit Lane, a name which conjures up bygone rural entertainment. It is signed to Petty Pool and Daleford Lane.

Beyond a small clutch of large houses the surface ends, the track enters woodland, keeping just inside the boundary. Immediately beyond a Portakabin on your right, and before a set of double iron gates, turn

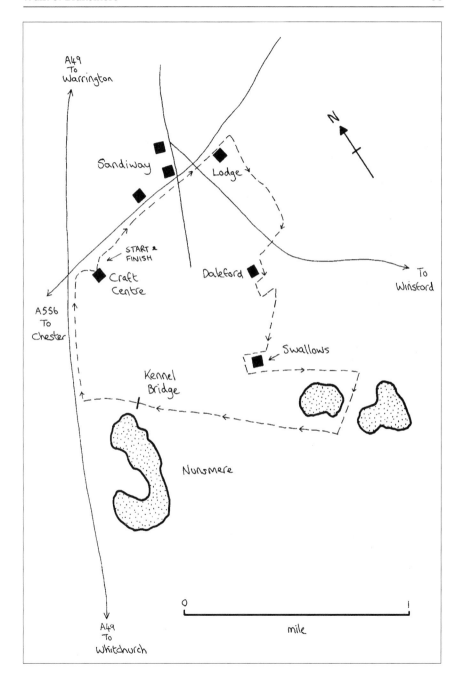

right over a waymarked stile and then immediately left as the path skirts a skid pan used by the Cheshire Constabulary when training drivers.

After 20 metres negotiate a second stile and turn right to walk alongside a fence on your right. There is a stream down below on your left. Immediately beyond an open (currently) decrepit metal five-barred gate on your right, look out for a waymark on the gatepost. Turn right and stay to the left of the wire fence for a few metres before corkscrewing left down through some trees to a stile which provides access to Daleford Lane.

Cross directly into a lane signed as a footpath to Kennel Lane. Keep the brick built Daleford Cottage on your left as you advance to a three-armed footpath post. Bear left, with the lane, to pass through Daleford Manor Caravan Park to reach Daleford Farm.

Continue with the track as it winds its way across open farmland to pass through the yard of Swallow Farm with its noisy pair of guard dogs until reaching a T-junction a few metres beyond.

Turn left along Kennel Lane as it heads eastwards through flanking holly trees. Soon, however, a large lake, created from abandoned sand workings, appears on the left. Continue until reaching a junction on the edge of Newchurch Common. Turn right so that you have another lake on your left and proceed to a waymarked stile after 30 metres. Maintain the same line of direction through some conifers.

Corner round the lake until reaching a stile in the fence on your right. Climb this onto the Whitegate Way, another of Cheshire's abandoned railway lines converted into a walking route.

Turn right, heading in a westerly direction across heathland dotted with innumerable pools with names such as "Shemmy Moss" and "Reeking Hole".

After more than a mile pass beneath Kennel Bridge to find Nunsmere, with Nunsmere Hall beyond, on your left. On approaching a second bridge, turn right up the flight of steps, to join the A49, Whitchurch to Warrington road. Turn right along this for approximately 500 metres to the traffic lights at the junction with the A556. Turn right and then, right again, along the path into the Blakemere Craft Centre.

𝒲𝒶𝓁𝓀 7. 𝒞𝑜𝓉𝑒𝒷𝓇𝑜𝑜𝓀

Route: Cotebrook – Little Budworth Common – Country Park – White Hall – Hawkswood – Beech Road – Coach Road – Hunter's Lodge – Cotebrook.

Start: The Coffee Shop, Cotebrook. Map reference 571655

Distance: 3¼ miles

Map: "Northwich & Delamere Forest", no. 267 in the O.S. Explorer series.

Public Transport: Cotebrook is served by daily (not Sunday) buses from Chester, Tarporley and Bunbury. There is one bus a day from Northwich on Tuesdays, Fridays and Saturdays.

By Car: Cotebrook is on the A49 between Sandiway and Tarporley. Parking is restricted. An alternative start is from the car park at Little Budworth Country Park, map reference 593654. This is located on the Coach Road which leaves the A49 north of Cotebrook and is signed to Little Budworth. The car park is opposite the entrance to Oulton Park.

The Tea Shop

Although the Coffee Shop is the official start of this walk, **Cotebrook Shire Horse Centre** is just 50 yards away on the busy A49 (next to The Alvanley Arms). Set in 50 acres of Cheshire countryside, complete with picnic area, it's a great place to visit before or after your walk – and there are also plans to open a café (but check first). Home of the internationally renowned Cotebrook Stud they have been breeding prize-winning shires here for over 30 years. They have also stocked the park with a fantastic selection of British animals and birdlife, both wild and domesticated, including many rare breeds.

Open: All year 10.00am to 5.00pm (every day except Tuesdays). Admission (in 2005): Adult £4.95, Concessions £3.95, Child £2.95, Family 2 + 3 children £14.50, Under 5 free. Phone: 01829 760506.

The **Coffee Shop at Cotebrook** closed for a while but we are pleased to report that it has re-opened and is now run by Sandra Smith. Based within a modern conservatory, the pine furniture helps to combine a bright atmosphere with a rural ambience.

There is a wide choice of cakes and other delights, all home-cooked. A traditional roast Sunday lunch will satisfy weekend walkers with larger appetites. Phone: 01829-760144 – other details overleaf.

The entrance to Oulton Park

Opening Hours: Daily 10 am to 4pm all year. Closed Mondays.

Little Budworth

The thatched cottages of this tiny out-of-the-way village surround the church with its medieval tower and gargoyles. The interior is mainly of Georgian design and houses various memorials to the Egerton family which lived at Oulton Park, now the motor racing circuit.

The woodlands outside the village are remnants of the hunting Forest of Mara and Mondrum which stretched from Frodsham to Nantwich. Our route crosses what is regarded as the finest example of lowland heath in Cheshire, noted for its woodcock, brown hare, butterflies, slippery jack fungus and damselflies.

Cotebrook derives its name from the Anglo-Saxon for an enclosure or fold for animals besides the brook.

The Route

From the Coffee Shop at Cotebrook head northwards along the busy A49 for approximately 100 metres. By the telephone kiosk branch off to the right over a stream into a narrow hedged lane which climbs for a further 150 metres before levelling out.

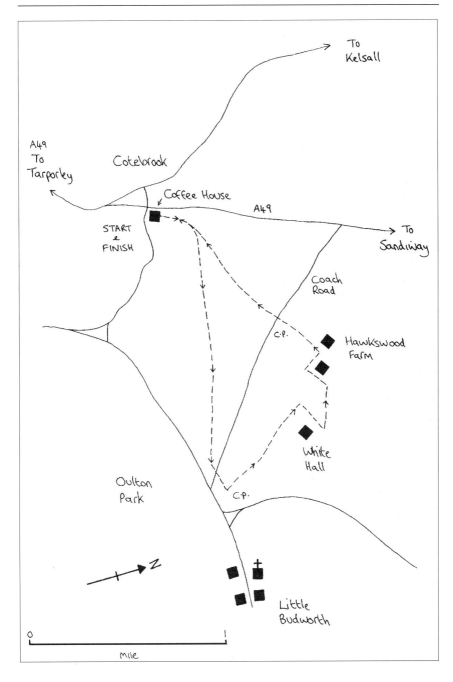

After a quarter of a mile this lane forms a T-junction with another. Ignore the junction. Instead make a right turn over a stile by a footpath finger post onto a field path signed to Little Budworth village.

Aim for the obvious stile in the facing hedgerow some 50 metres distant. Over that veer right up a slight rise and, on gaining the crown of a very large field, strike out for the stile which stands by a gateway and close to the corner of a hedge.

Beyond that, walk to the left of another hedgerow to a stile by a double five-barred metal gate. In the ensuing field remain to the left of the hedge to reach a stile adjacent to a single metal five-barred gate.

Using the waymark as the direction finder, curve a little to the left following a very obvious path to a stile alongside a wooden five-barred gate. This permits an exit onto a bridleway. Cross to the facing stile with a footpath sign.

Over this particular stile turn sharp right as the path weaves its course through the woodlands of Little Budworth Common. At the first intersection of paths keep the same line of direction until meeting a waymarked post. This is quickly followed by a T-junction.

Turn left to cross a small expanse of heathland to another intersection. This time stay forward, cross a bridleway but, at the next T-junction turn right. Then, almost immediately, go left onto a short path leading to the Coach Road. Cross this into the car park of Little Budworth Country Park.

A short digression of a hundred metres to the right will be rewarded by a view of the impressive classical main entrance to Oulton Park set against a backdrop of equally impressive beech trees. Exit the car park by taking the path to the right of the display panel. Wander through this remnant of the ancient Forest of Mara and Mondrum while keeping just inside the woodland boundary.

After some distance, pass to the right of a wooden five-barred gate to emerge onto a large area of heathland. Traverse this by following the clear path as it maintains the same line of direction, eventually crossing the metalled driveway leading to White Hall, a large redbrick and black and white building through the trees to your right.

On meeting a bridleway, a short distance beyond, turn right. At the junction by a set of two five-barred gates, make an acute turn to your left along a path signed to the Coach Road.

At the subsequent intersection in the middle of the woodland turn right. A Y-junction is reached after only a short distance. Fork right onto a broad path which dips as it passes a pool on your left before climbing to a stile. Having negotiated this, pass through the yard of Beech House Farm to emerge onto Beech Road. Turn left. To your right is "Hawkswood", a large cream-coloured house.

Pass another small car park on your left before reaching the Coach Road. Cross into the facing bridleway and, ignoring all paths leading off to right or left, follow the lane until well beyond Hunter's Lodge.

Where the lane bends round through ninety degrees to the right by a four-armed finger post, stay forward into the sunken country lane signed to Cotebrook. This forms part of the outward route so retrace your steps to the A49 where a left turn will lead to the Coffee Shop at Cotebrook.

Walk 8. Tarporley

Route: Tarporley – Cobbler's Cross – Portal Golf Course – Eaton – Lightfoot Lane – Oakland – Hill Farm – Heath Green – Forest Road – Tarporley.

Start: Car park behind the British Legion Club, Tarporley. Signed from the centre of Tarporley. Map reference 555624.

Distance: 5¼ miles.

Map: "Northwich & Delamere Forest", no. 267 in the O.S. Explorer series.

Public Transport: Tarporley is served by frequent buses daily (including Sundays) from Chester, Nantwich, Newcastle-under-Lyme and Hanley.

By Car: Tarporley (now by-passed) stands at the junction of the A49 Warrington to Whitchurch road with the A51 Chester to Nantwich road. Car park is signed from the main road through the village.

The Tea Shop

The Number 6 Coffee Shop in Tarporley's High Street has already established itself as a meeting place for locals and visitors alike. It has a plain, uncluttered atmosphere with a tiled floor and brick-faced servery. Decorations take the form of wheatsheaves and dried-flower arrangements.

There is a range of coffees available, the beans being freshly ground on the premises, and a number of speciality teas. The olde-world atmosphere of Tarporley's coaching past is maintained by the presence of toasted muffins on the menu. The proprietor, Carol Duncan, provides Welsh Rarebit made to her own recipe, toasted sandwiches or toasties, sandwiches, filled baguettes, Club Sandwiches and soup and roll in addition to an appetising and extensive range of cakes and gateaux.

Opening times: Monday to Friday, 9.30am to 5.00pm; Saturday 10.30am to 5.00pm; Sunday, 11.00am to 4.00pm; Tel: 01829 732021

Tarporley

When mentioned in Domesday Book as "Tarpolei", the village occupied a site close to the present by-pass, moving to its present location as the township flourished and developed into a market town, after receiving its first charter from Edward I.

In Burton Square, just north of Forest Road, you will find "Quarry Cottage", the only reminder that a quarry was once worked at this spot.

It was here that the 15-inch footprint of an amphibian was discovered in the stone, proof that this could have been Jurassic Park.

Tarporley's heyday came with the coaching era when several of its hostelries provided accommodation for travellers between Chester and London including Celia Fiennes, that inveterate wanderer and ancestor of Sir Ranulph Fiennes. Its most famous coaching inn is The Swan, which still stands in the High Street. It is the home of the Tarporley Hunt Club probably the oldest in the country. Until 1939 the village was also the venue for race meetings and a well-salted meat pie designed to encourage thirst was traditionally served under the large chestnut tree near the Rising Sun pub.

Cottage at Eaton

Although Tarporley has some splendid black and white buildings dating from Tudor times, the overall impression of the High Street is Georgian. St Helen's Church dates from the fourteenth century but was extensively restored in the nineteenth. It contains memorials to two local families, the Crewes and the Dones.

The Route

Leaving the car park by the entrance turn right into High Street. Proceed a few metres beyond the Post Office. Turn right into Park Road which is signed to the hospital.

It climbs gently to pass the hospital and Rathbone Park, a complex of newly built retirement homes. A few metres beyond these, where the road bends round to the right and by a school sign, stay forward through an old gateway onto a wide track.

After 10 metres negotiate a stile and continue along the same line of direction while remaining to the immediate right of the headland separating two large fields and passing a redundant stile by a large tree.

On arriving at a large brown house on your right, negotiate a small metal gate followed by a hedged path for 20 metres to emerge onto a narrow road at Cobbler's Cross.

Turn left for approximately 100 metres and, at the point where the road bend straightens out, fork right up an unsigned lane. Pass to the right of Arderne Hall to reach a stile after 150 metres.

Climb the short path cobbled with red sandstone sets before forking left to gain a T-junction. Turn right along the surfaced track which runs across Portal Golf Course, named after the farm which once occupied the site of the rather splendid club house.

Pass the goods entrance to the Club House and stay forwards until meeting a four-armed footpath post. Turn right to follow the track signed to Eaton as it sweeps round to the left of the Club House and Flaxyard Farm before progressing through an avenue of trees with views across the Cheshire Plain to the Peckforton and Bickerton Hills.

100 metres before a large sandstone bungalow with a white gate to its right, leave wide track by diverting right towards an obvious small ladder stile with an accompanying footpath finger post.

Exercising extreme caution, because there is a blind bend a few feet to the right, cross the road to a facing stile with another footpath sign adjacent. Over that stay to the right of a hedge to a ladder stile after 50 metres. Maintain your line of direction to another stile built in the traditional style.

Beyond this cling to the right of the hedge until approximately 70 metres beyond a metal five-barred gate on your left. Then negotiate a stile on the left before taking a line diagonally right, aiming for another stile, this time at the end of a rather thin looking hedge.

Over that turn left for 20 metres and then, by a gateway, turn right over another stile before turning left to traverse a very large field. Head for the gap between the end of a row of houses to the left and a small detached redbrick cottage to the right.

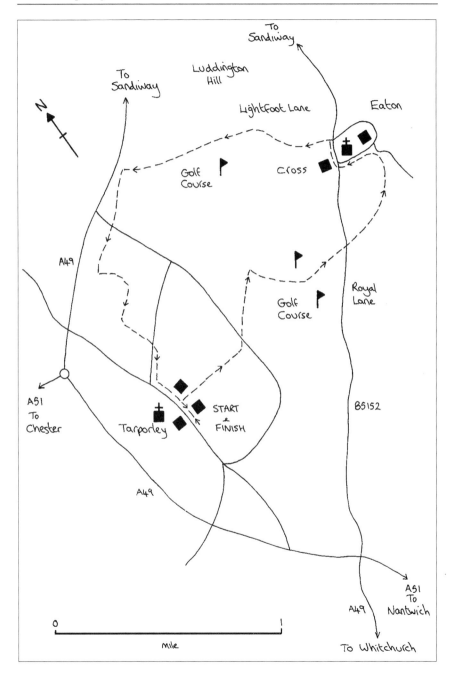

Between the two is a stile which provides access to a very narrow road. Turn left along this, passing the 30 mph signs after 10 metres and the Eaton village school to your right.

At the first junction stay forward into Edgewell Lane, lined mainly with modern property although "Well Cottage", a thatched, timber-framed, black and white house stands on your left. There is a similar style house almost directly opposite and both are not only attractive but are typical of the vernacular architecture of this particular area of central Cheshire.

At the subsequent T-junction make a right turn into Royal Lane to reach the sandstone cross with its eye-catching floral decorations in the centre of Eaton village.

Ignore Sapling Lane. However, opposite another thatched white house, "Silver Birches", stands an almost inconspicuous brick house. Over the front door is a stone tablet designed to resemble an open book. It reads,

> "God Is Truth
> The Word Is Truth
> The Spirit Is Truth
> Love Is Truth"

By the far corner of this house make a left turn into Lightfoot Lane. Although there is neither nameplate or sign at this junction, Lightfoot Lane is shown on the Ordnance Survey map.

Initially it climbs fairly steeply and the surface terminates by Knowl House. Beyond a conspicuous pair of locked lapwood gates it develops into a sunken lane as it ascends between hedgerows and with a surface of sandstone bedrock which, in turn, gives way to grass.

Oak, rowan, holly, ivy and bramble indicate that the hedgerows are of ancient origin suggesting that this may once have been an old packhorse route used for the transportation of salt. There is also an abundance of wild flowers in spring when wild garlic and celandine are to be seen while in summer it is the turn of foxglove, ragged robin, red campion and the ubiquitous rosebay willowherb.

The lane continues its upward course but the gradient eases before it reaches a T-junction. The lane leading off to the right heads for the Triangulation Pillar on Luddington Hill at 145 metres above sea level. Ignore this turn and the waymarks pointing to it. Instead turn left to emerge, within 100 metres, by the 9th tee of Oaklands Golf Course.

Stay with the wide sandy track to enjoy easy walking and an extensive vista across the north Cheshire Plain to your right. The occasional bench with a litter bin adjacent provides an ideal spot for a coffee break.

After a considerable distance over the golf course this track reaches the A49 by a metal five-barred gate. Turn left along the pavement. After 300 metres turn left down a side road signed to Tarporley. However, after a mere 20 metres, make a right turn into a lane to the immediate left of a five-barred gate and running parallel to the A49.

Stay to the right of a barn before losing height to a small metal gate with a bridleway sign adjacent. This provides access to a metalled lane which is closed-off to your immediate right by a set of bollards.

Turn left along this narrow road, Heath Green, soon passing Hill Farm on your right. Where the farm boundary fence ends, and by a footpath sign reading, "Forest Road, Utkinton Road", turn right over a stile.

Stay to the left of a fence to reach a stile in the far right-hand corner of the field. Then stay to the right of a row of large trees to a waymarked stile in the left-hand field corner. **Do not be tempted** by a stile some 50 metres to the right of this because it provides access **only** to a private garden.

Over the stile turn left as directed by the waymark, walking along the boundary of a cultivated field to a stile in the corner and then maintaining the same line to the right of a hedge with a view of the Welsh Hills to the west.

The path leads alongside "Lime House" to a stile adjacent to a metal five-barred gate. Turn right along Forest Road to meet High Street after 200 metres. Turn left for the walk through the village to your starting point, pausing for that afternoon tea in the Number 6 Coffee House on your way.

Walk 9. Higher Burwardsley

Route: Cheshire Workshops – Willow Hill Farm – Sandstone Trail – Bulkeley Hill – Sarra Lane – Cheshire Workshops.

Start: Cheshire Candle Workshops, Higher Burwardsley. Map reference 523565

Distance: 3 miles.

Map: "Crewe & Nantwich", no.257 in the O.S. Explorer series.

Public Transport: Burwardsley Post Office is served by daily buses from Chester, Whitchurch and Malpas. No Sunday service.

By Car: The Cheshire Workshops are signed from the A49 at Beeston and the A41 at Milton Green.

The Tea Shop

"The Granary", a small self-service cafe is part of the Cheshire Workshops complex. Anyone completing this walk by midday will be able to enjoy a bowl of hot, tasty soup accompanied by a crusty roll and followed by a light meal or salad. For the afternoon caller there is the usual Cheshire Cream Tea with scones, jam and tea, plus a large choice of tempting home-made cakes and gateaux.

Opening hours: Daily (including Sunday) 10.00am to 4.00pm; Phone: 01829 770401

Cheshire Workshops

Higher Burwardsley, a straggling village of stone cottages set on the flanks of the picturesque Peckforton Hills in central Cheshire, is the home of the Cheshire Candle Workshops. Founded in a small cottage in 1974 by Bob and Anne Sanderson, they moved to larger premises in 1978 but a disastrous fire in 1980 virtually gutted the building. Within a year, however, the new workshops had risen, phoenix-like from the ashes to become one of the most popular tourist attractions in the county.

In 1987 a change of ownership resulted in a new emphasis. While Richard James perpetuated the candle-making side of the business he introduced new crafts including glass blowing, pottery decoration and jewellery making. It proved enormously successful, attracting in excess of 200,000 visitors a year but financial problems resulted in a new management taking over in December 1994.

Visitors can watch demonstrations of candle making and even try their own hand at the craft. These are not the simple white sticks but elaborately shaped and highly decorated artistic creations, so beautiful that it seems like sacrilege to light one.

Opening times: Daily (including Sunday) 10.00 a.m. to 5.00 p.m.

The Route

Leaving the Candle Workshops car park by the official exit turn left along the narrow road for a few metres. Opposite "The Pheasant" and by a telephone kiosk, make an acute turn to the right, climbing a short, steep hill to reach a cross roads at the top.

Stay forward, even though there is a sign indicating that this road is a cul-de-sac. The gradient quickly levels out and the Cheshire Workshops appear on the far side of a field a hundred metres or so to the right.

Continue for approximately a quarter of a mile but, where the road bends sharply by the entrance to the driveway leading to Willow Hill Farm, stay with the surfaced lane by going round to the left.

After a short climb and by Fowler's Bench and Fowler's Lane, turn

Strange name – 'Meshach' at Higher Burwardsley (see page 52)

right, following the lane as it climbs yet again while opening-up a fine view over the plain towards the Welsh hills.

The surfaced lane terminates by the imposing red sandstone gate-house to Peckforton Castle. There, join the Sandstone Trail by turning right along the bridleway signed to Bulkeley Hill. The wide track passes between a stone wall on the right and mixed woodlands of birch, oak, beech and rowan on the left.

After a few hundred metres and by a footpath sign, turn left onto a steep, stepped path which initially has a hand rail on the right-hand side. Let the waymarks guide you as you climb steeply, twisting and turning for about half a mile through the woods which have an under storey of bracken, bramble and bilberry.

The summit of Bulkeley Hill is blessed with some fine specimens of oak and beech. The obvious path curves round the outside edge of this tree lined plateau before passing through a gateway in an old metal fence and then to the right of a fire hydrant and to the left of a small concrete building.

Beyond these landmarks the path loses altitude to a five-barred gate with a smaller metal one alongside on the boundary of the woodland.

Once through the gate swing right, as advised by the Sandstone Trail sign, following the well-trodden path over a field while staying a few metres to the right of a pylon.

Leave the field by an official gap to join Coppermine Lane. Cross into the facing lane which is signed to Rawhead Farm. A few metres before reaching "The Bungalow", with its barking dogs, and where the lane makes a sharp left turn towards Rawhead Farm, turn right over a stile to follow the path signed to Burwardsley.

Stay to the right of a wire fence which surrounds a small paddock. By the far corner of this, turn left over a waymarked stile and, keeping the fence on your left, descend a cultivated field. Pass beneath two lines of overhead wires before reaching a stile with a footpath sign. The attractive formation of Raw Head is clearly visible to your left.

Beyond the stile maintain direction, guided by the arm of the footpath finger post and also by the line of white posts erected by the farmer after removing hedgerows. In doing so you will pass to the left of a redundant stile and a large concrete water trough.

Over the next stile pass through a belt of trees some 50 metres wide to a footbridge. At the far end, turn left and then right and using the waymarks as direction finders, pass along the shallow valley staying just to the right of a stream until gaining another stile after some 200 metres.

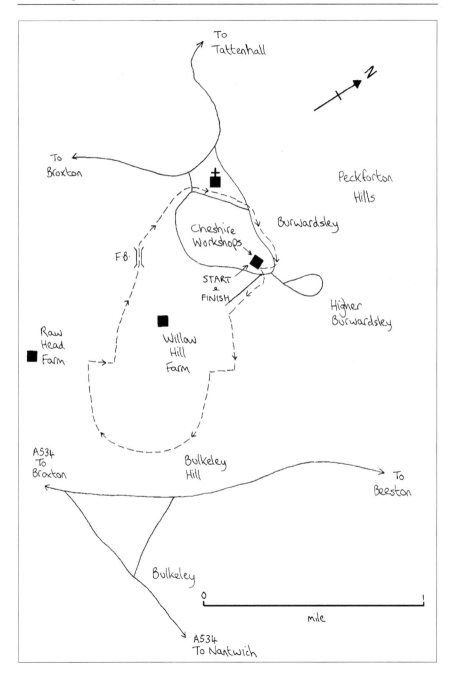

This provides an exit onto Sarra Lane. Turn left up the hill before the lane levels to reach a T-junction opposite St John's Church.

Turn right so that the church is on your left. Beyond Cheshire County Council's Field Study Centre the road dips into a hollow before climbing to pass "Aqueduct Cottage" on your left and the tree-covered slopes of Willow Hill on your right.

At the following road junction turn right. Along this stretch of road are three of the most unusually named cottages in Cheshire. They are "Bel Shazar", "Shadrach" and "Meshach". Another building of note is the tiny Methodist Church which was built of red sandstone in 1843.

At the subsequent junction make a right turn into the car park of the Cheshire Candle Workshops.

𝒲𝒶𝓁𝓀 10. 𝒫ℯ𝒸𝓀𝒻ℴ𝓇𝓉ℴ𝓃

Route: Beeston Castle – Moathouse Farm – Stanner Nab – Peckforton Castle – Peckforton Hall – Spurstow – Beeston Moss – Beeston Castle.

Start: Car park, Beeston Castle. Map reference 541592

Distance: 7 miles.

Map: "Crewe & Nantwich", no. 257 in the O.S. Explorer series.

Public Transport: Buses daily to Beeston village from Chester, Tarporley and Nantwich. (Not Sundays)

By Car: Beeston Castle is well-signposted from the A49 Warrington to Whitchurch road at Beeston Lock, about two miles south of Tarporley.

The Tea Shop

Surprisingly there is no café or tea shop at Beeston Castle or in Beeston village. The only place of refreshment is the Coffee Shop in Peckforton Castle. Housed in the former stables, grain store and coach house, this self-service restaurant offers a wide range of food from substantial lunches to light snacks. These can either be eaten inside the stables or, if the weather is fine, at one of the many tables in the castle yard.

As befits a stately mansion the fare is home-baked and there is nothing more relaxing than sitting in the grand surroundings while enjoying a scone smothered in local cream and jam followed by a cup of freshly brewed tea.

Opening hours: 10.00am to 5.00pm from 14th April to 10th September. Phone: 01829 260930.

Peckforton Castle

Seen from a distance, the battlements of Peckforton Castle standing above the trees, give it the appearance of a fairytale castle that we all dream about. In reality it is the nineteenth century creation of John Tollemache, MP for Cheshire, who was elevated to the peerage as Baron Tollemache in 1876. Designed by Anthony Salvin, it was built of local stone between 1844 and 1851.

It was described by Sir Gilbert Scott as "The largest and most carefully and learnedly executed Gothic mansion of the present day. It is not only a castle in name but it is a real and carefully constructed medi-

The entrance to Beeston Castle

eval fortress, capable of standing a siege from an Edwardian army." It was used for the filming of "Robin Hood, Prince of Thieves".

Beeston Castle

Standing on top of a crag high above the Cheshire plain, Beeston Castle enjoys a commanding position with views of the Welsh hills, the Pennines and even the Wrekin in Shropshire. The present castle dates from the thirteenth century when it was built by Ranulf, Earl of Chester, to protect his lands from the marauding Welsh.

It later passed into the ownership of the Crown and was used to house prisoners captured during the Welsh wars. It was thought impregnable until captured from the Roundheads by a group of Royalists during the Civil War. Today it is in the care of English Heritage, its extensive ruins being well worth a visit either before or after the walk.

Opening hours: 1st April to 31st October, daily, 10.00 a.m. to 6.00 p.m; 1st November to 31st March, daily, 10.00 a.m. to 4.00 p.m.

The Route

From the car park facing the entrance to Beeston Castle turn left along the narrow road but, after some 50 metres and where the road bends to the left, stay forward, keeping to the right of the picnic area.

Pass the Sandstone Trail notice board to a through stile waymarked with the logo of the Trail, a letter "S" on the sole of a walking boot. Continue for 100 metres with the boundary wall of the castle on your right and a hedge on your left. At the first Y-junction fork left, as signed, losing altitude through the woodland which consists principally of pine trees. At the bottom of the slope a stile provides access to Wickson Lane.

Cross diagonally left to a path signed to Grindley Brook. Keeping "Tabernacle Cottage" on your right, follow the wide path across the field while enjoying some excellent walking on a sandy surface which is gentle on the feet.

Cross the wooden footbridge spanning a tiny stream followed, after 20 metres, by a stile. Maintain direction across another field until gaining a stile with a footpath finger post alongside pointing the Sandstone Trail towards Bulkeley Hill.

Turn right along the private road to pass firstly Moathouse Barn and then, secondly, Moathouse Farm, both on your right. 150 metres beyond the latter, and by a small sandstone cottage, veer left up a wide track, still signed as a stretch of the Sandstone Trail. This climbs steeply through the woods of the Peckforton Estate with woodpeckers drumming and wrens calling from the undergrowth beneath the oaks, hollies, beeches and rowans. Where the track bends round to the right, the going eases to allow the path to run along the contour.

Eventually, after passing through a gateway an intersection in the path network is reached. Turn left for the steep and stepped climb up the flank of Peckforton Hill to Stenner Nab, reaching a T-junction on the crest.

Turn left, as directed by a waymarker and, after 50 metres and by a footpath sign, turn right. A gradual descent follows. Pass another footpath sign and, just beyond, negotiate a waymarked gap in the fence, continuing to lose height until meeting the main driveway to the castle. Turn left, up the drive, to the castle and tea shop.

Afterwards, return down the driveway, continuing through the turreted gateway and reaching the road. Turn right but, by the far corner of "Castle Cottage" which is on your left, make a sharp left turn into a lane. Stay with this for some considerable distance until, having passed to the right of Peckforton Hall, you reach Peckforton Hall Lane by a footpath finger post.

Turn left following this narrow and quiet surfaced road into the village of Spurstow. Pass the entrance to Southcroft with its village notice board and red telephone kiosk.

A short distance beyond, at a minor cross roads, turn left into a narrow road recognised by a footpath sign indicating a path to Beeston. Pass to the right of the Methodist Chapel, a red brick building dating from 1844. Beyond the first gateway the road develops into an unsurfaced track. Stay to the left of Haycroft Farm to a waymarked wooden stile adjacent to a metal five-barred gate. With Peckforton Castle directly ahead in the distance, advance a further 100 metres to a rusty five-barred gate.

Do not go through. Rather, veer away from the hedge to a small clump of trees. Pass through these to another gate. Again do not pass through. Instead go to the right so that the hedge is on your left. At the far end of the field go through a gap by a holly tree and continue alongside the hedge. In the far left-hand corner of this field negotiate a wooden stile adjacent to a small wooden gate which is partially obscured by the vegetation and a hedgerow.

Over the stile, maintain the line of direction but now along a narrow hedged lane which, after the first house, acquires a surface of loose chippings. Stay with this lane until it meets a road by a footpath sign at Beeston Moss. Turn right. After 200 metres and by the far corner of two very small brick cottages and 100 metres before a very large black and white house, turn left over a wooden stile onto a path signed to Beeston and Beeston Brook.

Walk to the right of a hedgerow to a waymarked double stile in the field corner. Over either of these fork left, as indicated by a waymark, to traverse an arable field. The path is far from clear so aim for a small clump of trees roughly midway between Peckforton and Beeston Castles.

Negotiate the stile in the facing hedgerow before maintaining the same line of direction across a smaller cultivated field. After the next stile turn right, walking to the left of a hedge. Where this corners away to the right, continue forward, heading for the side of a brick house ahead.

After negotiating another stile, again with a footpath sign adjacent, cross the footbridge to gain the road. Turn right to a T-junction after 100 metres. Turn left into a road so narrow it is provided with passing places. Continue along this to another T-junction facing the wall of Beeston Castle. Make a left turn for the final 100 metres to the car park from which you started.

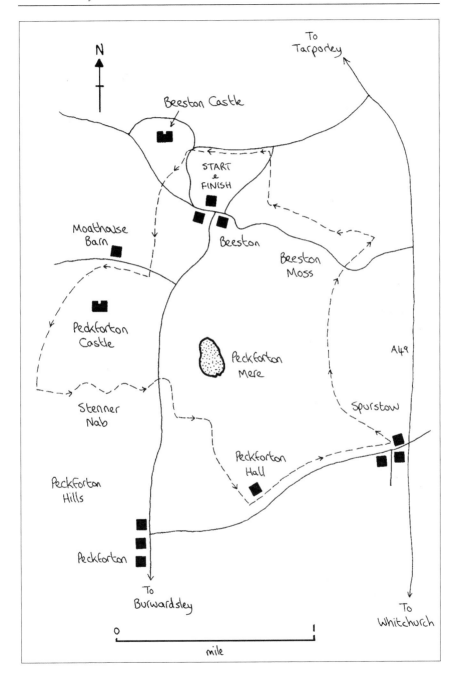

N

To
Tarporley

Beeston Castle

START
&
FINISH

Moathouse
Barn

Beeston

Beeston
Moss

Peckforton
Castle

Peckforton
Mere

A49

Stenner
Nab

Spurstow

Peckforton
Hall

Peckforton
Hills

Peckforton

To
Burwardsley

To
Whitchurch

0   mile

Walk 11. Audlem

Route: Audlem – Shropshire Union Canal – Cox Bank – Adderley Pool – Hawksmoor – Highfields Farm – Kinseyheath – Wood Orchard Lane – Sandy Lane – Audlem.

Start: The car park off Cheshire Road, Audlem. Map reference 659437

Distance: 6 miles.

Map: "Crewe & Nantwich", no. 257 in the O.S. Explorer series.

Public Transport: Audlem is served by frequent daily buses (Not Sunday) from Whitchurch and Nantwich. There is a restricted service from Crewe. On Saturdays there is a service from Hanley.

By Car: Audlem may be reached by the A525 from Newcastle-under-Lyme and Whitchurch and the A529 from Nantwich and Market Drayton. There is a large free car park off Cheshire Street near the village centre.

The Tea Shop

The Old Priest House in Vicarage Lane is probably the most quaint of all the cafes included in this collection. The house itself is of uncertain date but has been in existence for more than 500 years according to Andrew Halliwell who has co-owned it since November, 1993.

There is a small single room with old-fashioned red and blue quarry tiles on the floor, circular tables with some spindle-backed chairs and a genuine old wooden-backed settle.

There is nothing old-fashioned about the fare they provide. In addition to a selection of light meals including Staffordshire Oatcakes with various fillings, they serve afternoon teas with scones lavishly covered in local cream and offer a bewildering array of home-made cakes.

One speciality of the house is ice cream, produced on the premises, which has given birth to a special ice-cream menu. Coffee and tea are freshly brewed and served in either cafetieres or large pots. It is an experience not to be missed and makes the perfect conclusion to any walk.

Opening hours: 9.00am to 5.00pm, closed Tuesdays. Phone: 01270 811749.

Important Note: closed due to fire in March 2005 – we hope that repairs will enable the establishment to reopen as soon as possible. Meanwhile, one of the two pubs in the vollage will make you welcome.

Audlem

Audlem, undoubtedly one of the most picturesque villages in Cheshire, is located in the deep south of the county very close to the boundary with Shropshire. At 360 feet above sea level, it lies in the core of the county's pastoral countryside, being noted for its dairy products including Cheshire Cheese. Many of these may still be purchased in the village shops.

Formerly it was an important wharf on the Shropshire Union Canal which today caters only for pleasure craft. Nevertheless Audlem, sitting at the foot of a flight of 15 locks which carry the waterway down from the Shropshire Heights to the Cheshire Plain, is an important mooring area with canalside pubs and a canalside shop.

Audlem is very unusual, perhaps unique, in that the main roads leading away from the central square, all bear the names of the counties to which they lead – Cheshire, Staffordshire and Shropshire.

The focal point of this village or small town is the sturdy, square-towered parish church of St James the Great, built originally about 1200 but enlarged in the fourteenth century and renovated as recently as 1994.

It has several items of Tudor and Jacobean interest including the

Audlem

chancel roof and the pulpit. Close by the doorway is the ancient maypole crown and in the small chapel is a Roman funeral urn which has been dated between 70 and 80 AD.

Standing in front of the church is the Buttercross, built in 1733 and used by the local farmers for selling butter and cheese until 1914. Audlem was granted a market charter by Edward I in 1295 and continued to hold its weekly market until the outbreak of the First World War.

The village is full of other interesting buildings and, after the walk, it is well worth while having a saunter through the streets with a guide leaflet which is available for a small charge from the Old Priest's House.

The Route

From the car park entrance turn right into Cheshire Street for the 150 metres to the village centre. The church of St James the Great, the Buttercross and the Bear Stone are all on your left.

The Bear Stone is a piece of granite, believed to have originated in Cumbria, which was carried south during the Ice Age before being deposited in Audlem. For decades it was used as a tethering post for the bears while they were baited by dogs.

By the Lord Combermere Hotel, a black and white building, turn right into Shropshire Street. After 200 metres and by the Bridge Inn, turn right, as signed, for the Wharf where a left turn down a short flight of steps leads onto the canal towpath.

Make another left turn and, with the canal on your right, pass under the bridge to emerge into a landscape which is lush, green, rolling and pastoral, the very essence of rural Cheshire. The path climbs alongside a series of locks before passing under Bridge number 77.

More locks follow, plus a milestone indicating that Nantwich is seven miles distant, Norbury Junction 16½ miles and Autherley Junction 32. Mallard and moorhen grace the water while it is not uncommon to observe a heron either flying overhead or standing motionless on the bank.

By bridge number 76 the gradient levels out while the path acquires a grass surface which is gentle on the feet. Remain with the canal, crossing the boundary into Shropshire shortly beyond the bow bridge which carries Bagley Lane overhead.

A long straight stretch carries you to Castle Hill, where formerly a Motte and Bailey castle occupied the site. A short distance beyond Pool House and Adderley Pool Bridge you approach Hawksmoor Bridge. A few metres before reaching it, however, go left up the short flight of

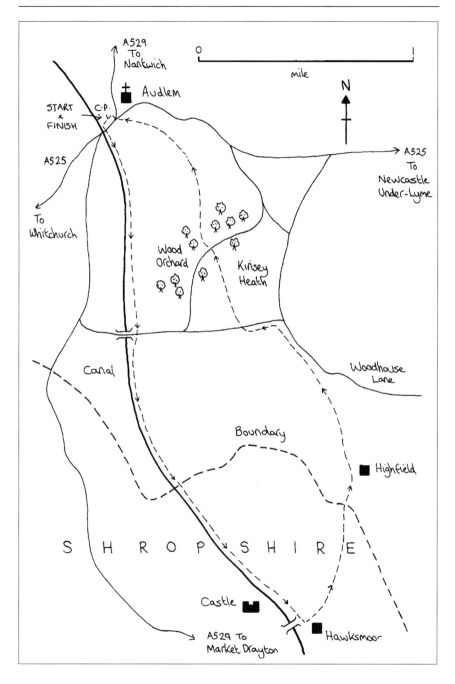

steps and negotiate the small metal gate to make a left turn along the approach road to Hawksmoor Farm. The farmhouse is a stately, well-proportioned and elegant building in red brick.

Pass to the left of the farmhouse but continue forward through the middle of the stockyard with its enormous covered pens and two metal gates. The concrete track soon develops into a wide unsurfaced lane flanked by hedgerows and, especially after wet weather, can be very muddy.

In due course the hedges are replaced by fencing on both sides before a metal five-barred gate signals the end of the lane. Beyond, maintain direction to the right of an electric fence, proceeding through a wide avenue of oaks while traversing a landscape resembling a parkland as the county boundary slips unnoticed under your boots.

Soon Highfields Farm which is noted for its herd of English Holsteins, comes into view a short distance away to the right. This imposing half-timbered black and white mansion is the first house in Cheshire.

Along this grassy path notice the gnarled stump of a tree on your left. It is reminiscent of a Henry Moore Sculpture except that this has been fashioned by nature.

With Highfields Farm away to your right, and by a clump of broad-leaved trees, pass through an official gap in the fence to meet the wide track which comes from the farm. Turn left along this, cross a cattle grid and remain with it until reaching an inverted Y-junction recognised by a small, white-painted boulder. On it is an arrow pointing to "Floristry and Country Salon".

Turn left, proceeding along the level track until meeting Woodhouse Lane by a black and white house. Go left along the narrow road for approximately a quarter of a mile to reach a T-junction.

Turn left into Bagley Lane which is signposted to Swansbach and Market Drayton. Opposite Kinseyheath Farm and by a footpath finger post, turn right over a stile to advance to the right of the boundary fence of Kinsey House, a white affair carrying the date 1902.

Beyond the next stile, set into a facing hedge, make a direct line for the left-hand corner of the field. Turn left over the stile and then turn immediately to the right.

Walk to the left of the boundary hedge of a cultivated field, following it round the first corner. By the second corner negotiate a stile before keeping forward as directed by the waymark. Initially the path is clear and well-used as you aim for a distant house with a long row of chimney pots. However, having passed under some overhead wires, veer right towards a hedge corner and then keep a hedge on your left until the next waymarked stile by a wooden finger post.

This stile provides access to Orchard Wood Lane. Cross directly to a facing footpath sign. Keeping to the right of a tiny red brick cottage, proceed along a broad track.

Look out on your left for a giant willow rising from what was obviously a pond and, just beyond, ignore the left turn to Fields Farm. Remain along the lane until, a short distance after Sandy Lane Farm, you reach a junction. Turn left over the stile adjacent to a footpath finger post. Taking your direction from the arm of the post, cross a large field to the hedge corner on the right.

Continue to the left of this hedge to a stile. This permits access to a tiny village green, once the traditional site for a maypole. Cross it to reach Vicarage Lane opposite the tiniest house in Audlem and the rather more imposing Old Grammar School.

Now an old people's home, it is a building of the Stuart period dating from 1646 and paid for by three rich local people. It remained a grammar school until the early years of this century, re-opening as a mixed senior School in 1913 and remaining in use as an educational establishment until 1965.

Opposite the Grammar School turn left along Vicarage Lane. Climb the short distance to the Old Priest's House and welcome refreshments before crossing the Square into Cheshire Street and returning to the car park.

Walk 12. Bridgemere

Route: Bridgemere – Phynsons Hayes – Checkley Wood – Checkley – Bank Farm – Bridgemere.

Start: Bridgemere Garden Centre on the A51 between Nantwich and Woore. Map reference 725436.

Distance: 5½ miles.

Map: "Crewe & Nantwich", no. 257 in the O.S. Explorer series.

Public Transport: None

By Car: The Bridgemere Garden Centre is on the A51 south of Nantwich and north of Woore, approximately 100 metres north of the boundary between Cheshire and Shropshire. Large car park for patrons.

The Tea Shop

The Coffee Shop at the Bridgemere Garden Centre is recommended by no less an authority than Egon Ronay for the quality of its food. Breakfasts and light lunches are served in the bright and airy cafe located inside the garden centre. In addition there is a bewildering array of scones, gateaux and cakes, all home-made, along with a selection of speciality teas and coffees. It is self service.

Opening hours: Daily, 9.00 a.m. to dusk in summer; Daily, 9.00am to 5.00pm in winter; tel: 01270 521100

Bridgemere Garden World

John Ravenscroft launched Bridgemere Garden World in the early 1960s cultivating roses on three acres of land by the roadside. Today the centre, the largest of its kind in Europe, covers 250 acres. It also includes Garden Kingdoms, a display of over 20 types of garden including one in the French style, a Victorian model and the Chelsea Gold Medal winners. Fuelled by inspiration, a visit to the commercial sections will prove irresistible.

The Route

Leaving Bridgemere Garden World by the car park exit, turn right along the A51 but, after 200 metres and by the far end of a brick cottage and a waymarker post, turn right again this time into a hedged lane.

Within about 300 metres, and by a footpath sign, turn right through a

Thatched cottage at Checkley

five-barred metal gate before bearing slightly left towards an obvious waymarker post. Stay to the right of this and also of a subsequent row of oak trees to descend to a stile in a very shallow valley.

At the far end of a wooden footbridge spanning the brook veer right through a narrow belt of trees whilst climbing gently for 15 metres to another stile.

Over that turn sharply to the right to walk along the boundary of a very large field with a wood on your immediate right. At this point the landscape is gently undulating and well-wooded with large numbers of pheasants wandering freely. In the far corner of this field negotiate a stile before bearing left, as per the waymark, to a white metal gate with a footpath sign adjacent.

Pass through the yard of Phynsons Hayes Farm and then bear left along a wide cinder track which is waymarked. In the very far distance ahead is the unmistakable outline of Mow Cop near Congleton.

Having passed through a gateway with a five-barred metal gate hanging uselessly from one post, there is a tree-lined pond on your right which boasts a large population of Mallard. From this spot on a clear day it is possible to see the Peckforton Hills, and beyond them, the Clywydian Hills of Wales.

After some considerable distance pass to the right of an elevated green fuel tank before going through a waymarked blue metal five-barred gate. After 100 metres there is a gas pipeline marker on your left. By this stage the lane has lost its open aspect, having acquired hedgerows of oak, hawthorn and willow on both sides. Checkley Wood is but a field's distance away to your left.

Stay with the track as it negotiates three sets of blue double five-barred gates in quick succession and twists its way to the left of Checkley Wood Farm before acquiring a metalled surface.

After a considerable distance, and by Checkley Wood Cottages, turn left along the concrete drive leading to New Checkley Wood Farm. Stay to the left of the farmhouse but through the centre of the yard as directed by a series of waymarks and signs. After leaving the farm the track loses its surface as it runs between two lines of electric fence, erected to control the grazing of the large herds of cattle.

When the track terminates stay forward across the centre of the very large field while aiming for some distant cottages and passing by a wooden waymarker post standing by some zinc cattle troughs on the way. On approaching, make a line for the blue gate to the right of the cottages to reach the road. Ignore the waymark which points right and is giving directions for a much longer walk. Instead make a left turn along the road through Checkley hamlet.

Look for the attractive thatched cottages and Checkley Hall as you walk through. A slight climb will bring you to a house on the left bearing a plaque which reads: "DLB 1907". By this, turn left into a narrow surfaced lane which is signed as a cul-de-sac. Pass to the right of Bank Farm and look out for "Cherry Tree Cottage" which has an old-fashioned hand pump in its garden.

100 metres beyond this, turn right over a stile but ignore the direction of the footpath arm. Rather, bear left over a cultivated field to pass close by a pylon before descending into a hollow where there is a waymarked stile. Beyond, and following the distinctive path, continue forward over the hump in the centre of a meadow to negotiate a narrow footbridge before heading up the slope to a stile alongside another footpath sign.

Advance to the second stile after six metres, cross another footbridge, negotiate the stile at the far end and then turn left. Almost immediately turn right to walk to the left of a hedge. After several metres swing right, with the path, as it passes through the hedgerow to join a lane which carries you to a waymarked stile by a five-barred metal gate.

This provides access to a lane. Turn left to pass Bridgemere Farm before, some distance beyond, re-joining your outward route back to Bridgemere Garden World.

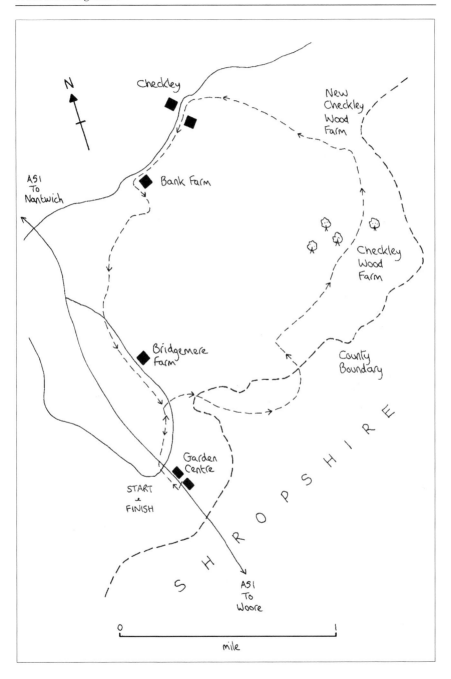

Walk 13. Nantwich

Route: Nantwich – Welshmen's Lane – Shropshire Union Canal – Green Lane – Nantwich Lake – Nantwich.

Start: Hilton's Tea Rooms, Beam Street, Nantwich. Map reference 652525

Distance: 4 miles.

Map: "Crewe & Nantwich", no. 257 in the O.S. Explorer series.

Public Transport: Nantwich Station has direct rail services from Chester, Crewe, Whitchurch, Shrewsbury, Hereford, Newport and Cardiff. Daily including Sundays. In addition to local services Nantwich has daily (including Sunday) buses from Hanley, Newcastle-under-Lyme, Crewe, Tarporley and Chester. Frequent daily buses from Audlem and Whitchurch (Not Sundays).

By Car: Nantwich may be reached by the A530 from Whitchurch and Middlewich, the A529 from Audlem and Market Drayton, the A51 from Chester and Stone, the A500 from Stoke and Newcastle, the A534 from Crewe and Wrexham, and the A500 from Junction 16 on the M6 Motorway. There are several signed car parks in the town centre.

The Tea Shop

Run by Sheila Ashley and Janet Soames, Hilton's Tea Rooms in Beam Street, Nantwich, offers a wide range of light meals, salads, sandwiches and baked potatoes. Their speciality is Norfolk Shortcake made to a secret recipe but there is also a tempting range of home-baked gateaux and cakes. Afternoon teas complete with scones, jam and cream and fruit cakes are perhaps the best way to round off this short walk. Not surprisingly they offer excellent pots of tea and cups of coffee.

Opening hours: Daily 9.30am to 4.00pm. Closed Sundays. Phone 01270 611488

Nantwich

Nantwich started life as Hellath Wen, meaning "Salt Pit" before the Anglo-Saxon invasions resulted in a name change to Warmundestrou. Under the Normans it became Wich Malbanc, later changed to Namtwych which, in turn, has been corrupted into the present name.

It was salt which laid the foundations of the town's lasting prosperity from Roman times until the nineteenth century. By this time it had de-

Tudor façade, Nantwich

veloped into an important market town for South Cheshire with boot and shoe manufacture and glove making adding to its wealth.

The Great Fire of 1583 lasted for 20 days, destroying much of the existing town. It also provided an excellent opportunity for re-building, towards the cost of which Queen Elizabeth I contributed. Some of the oak beams which she sent gave their name to the present Beam Street.

Often referred to as "The Cathedral of South Cheshire", because of its size, the parish church of St Mary well repays a visit. This is not the place to provide a detailed description because there are numerous guides on sale within the church itself.

Many of the sixteenth century black and white buildings survive, providing Nantwich with its unique atmosphere and have led to its being classified as one of this country's 51 Town Preservation Sites. Many of the buildings are passed on this walk.

Town guides are available from the Tourist Information Centre, Church House, The Square.

The Route

From Hilton's Tea Rooms turn right to walk along Beam Street towards the town centre, bending round to the left as it develops into a modern shopping precinct with Boots the Chemists on your right.

At the first junction make a right turn into High Street to reach Water Lode. Cross directly by the traffic lights to enter Welsh Row, the street once used by Welsh cattle drovers coming into Nantwich for salt.

The Row was formerly part of the main road from London to Wales during the coaching era and was also used by the Royalist Army on its approach to Nantwich during the Civil War.

Close by the bridge over the River Weaver at the entrance to Wood Street is the site of the original salt spring which supplied salt to the Roman garrison and continued in use until the nineteenth century.

Continue along Welsh Row but, by the far corner of Grocott's Garage, turn right by a footpath sign into King's Lane, passing between fences to a stile after 100 metres. Continue forward to the right of a hawthorn hedge before veering slightly to the right to another stile which is located about 50 metres to the right of the field corner. Over that, turn through ninety degrees to the left, staying close-in to the hedge on your left and then turning right in the first field corner.

By the second field corner turn left over a small planked footbridge. At the far end turn right over a stile. Proceed to the right of a hedge and in the next corner turn right over another footbridge before advancing to a stile in another field corner.

Continue forward, still to the left of a hedge until reaching a wooden five-barred gate which provides an exit onto Welshman's Lane. Turn left along this quiet surfaced road for about 250 metres until arriving at a redbrick cottage standing where the lane bends sharply to the left. There, turn right between the black and white bollards onto a narrow path which climbs the embankment onto the towpath of the Shropshire Union Canal.

Turn left along the towpath crossing Chester Road by means of the Nantwich Aqueduct and continuing by the canal moorings where several narrow boats are tied up. Many of these have elaborate decorations and enjoy such names as "Woven Grass", "Topas", "Peregrine" and "Elysium".

There is open country to both left and right but the far bank is tree-lined. Mallard may be seen swimming while the numbers of anglers on the banks testify to the abundance of fish. There is also a view of Acton Church to the right and of Nantwich Church to the left.

Walk under the arched stone bridge carrying Marsh Lane over the canal and pass the milestone which announces, "Nantwich 1 mile, Autherley Junction 38 miles and Norbury Junction 22½ miles".

On reaching Green Lane Bridge pass underneath before making an

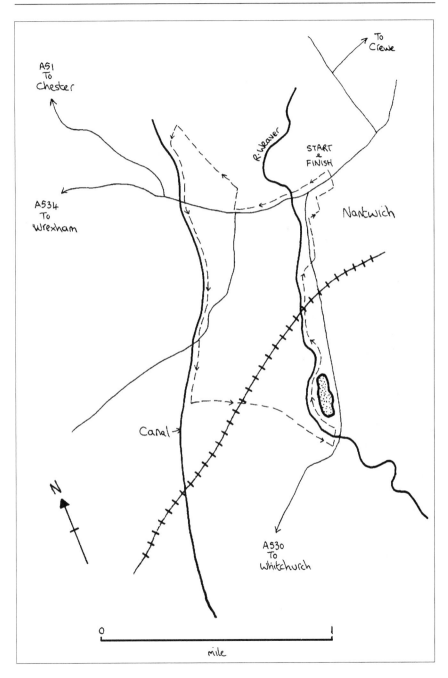

acute left turn up the bank to Green Lane. Cross to a small metal gate alongside a five-barred one complete with a bridleway sign.

Go through the small gate and, with your back to the canal, walk to the left of a hedge. Pass to the left of a tree-surrounded pond and through another small metal gate and continue between a wooden fence on your left and a hedge on your right to a small wooden gate. Through this cross the railway line to another small gate and maintain direction through a waymarked five-barred gate. Negotiate a small metal gate into some sheep pens and exit by a five-barred one to follow a well-maintained path which crosses a wooden footbridge before reaching the A530, a few metres to the left of Shrewbridge House.

Turn left along the main road but, after 100 metres, turn left again over an area of open grassland to a footbridge spanning the River Weaver some 50 metres from the road. At the far end turn right along the path with Nantwich Lake between you and the A530.

Beyond the far end of the lake keep to the left of a specially created wildflower meadow to the memorial to Flight Lieutenant Arthur Brown of the United States Army Air Force who, on January 14th, 1944, stayed at the controls of his Thunderbolt fighter plane to avoid crashing onto Nantwich town centre with the possibility of a major loss of life. A native of New York, he was only 23 years-old when he performed this heroic act for which the inhabitants of Nantwich will be forever grateful. From this point onwards the path acquires a surface and passes beneath the railway before reaching a T-junction. Fork right to regain the A530.

Turn left along this to the traffic island where a left fork leads into Water Lode. At the first junction make a right turn into Mill Street where several mills have stood since the one recorded in the Domesday Book of 1086.

At the far end of Mill Street turn left along Pillory Street and pass the parish church of St Mary into High Street before forking right into Churchyardside. On emerging make a left turn into Pepper Street which leads you directly to Beam Street and your starting point.

Walk 14. Hassall Green

Route: Vistra Marina – M6 Motorway – Woody Fields – Malkin's Bank – Trent and Mersey Canal – Vistra Marina.

Start: Vistra Marina, Hassall Green. Map reference 772584

Distance: 3 miles.

Map: "Crewe & Nantwich", no. 257 in the O.S. Explorer series.

Public Transport: Hassall Green has daily buses (not Sunday) from Sandbach, Alsager and Hanley.

By Car: Hassall Green is on a minor road which is signed from the A533 south of Sandbach and from Wheelock Heath on the A534. There is a car park at the Vistra Marina, otherwise use roadside parking.

The Tea Shop

The former Lockside Tea Room at Hassall Green has been transformed into Brindley's Lockside Restaurant and is well patronised by the boating fraternity as well as locals. There are several reasons for this, not least being the fact that the lock is about midway up the flight of thirty which elevates the Trent and Mersey Canal from the Cheshire Plain to Stoke-on-Trent. So what better place to pause for a mid-morning coffee or Afternoon Tea, sitting inside or at one of the many tables on the green outside idly watching the boats sail by.

The restaurant, which is upstairs, is housed in a building that dates from 1766 and served originally as a stable and hay store for horses once used for hauling the barges. It was also a shop for the Navvies who could spend their company tokens there. The walls are red brick, although one by way of contrast, has been painted green and the roof is supported by thick wooden beams.

The furniture is solid, stout wooden tables being partnered by spindle-backed chairs. The view through the windows is of the locks and the undulating Cheshire countryside with traffic roaring along the M6 Motorway only a short distance away.

There is a very extensive lunchtime and evening menu embracing such dishes as baked goat's cheese with mango and chives or deep-fried Calamari for starters. Main courses include a variety of steaks or chicken and whisky casserole on a bed of rice. Full English Breakfasts are served from 9.45am until 11am.

The Brindleys building alongside the Shropshire Union Canal

For anyone in search of something lighter there is a wonderful display of home-made cakes and gateaux, scones with jam and cream or the traditional Afternoon Tea. All may be accompanied by speciality teas and coffees.

Opening hours: Weekdays: all year 9.45am to 5pm.(last food order 4.30 pm.) Evening meals from 7.00pm to 9.30pm. Tel: 01270 762 266.

The Route

From the Vistra Marina turn right along the road leading away from the Trent and Mersey Canal and heading towards the village of Hassall Green. At the first road junction by the "Romping Donkey" pub stay forward along the road signed to Smallwood. A small estate of houses, "The Paddock", is on your left.

At the second road junction, within 100 metres of the first, stay forward again but only for a few metres before turning left into Charles Square. Walk about 50 metres along the approach road to enter the actual square which is surrounded by houses. Cross diagonally to the left-hand corner where a signed footpath leaves the square between houses numbered 55 and 57. It reaches a stile after 50 metres.

Beyond this take the well-defined path across the centre of the field towards the M6 Motorway. Negotiate a stile in the far corner and turn

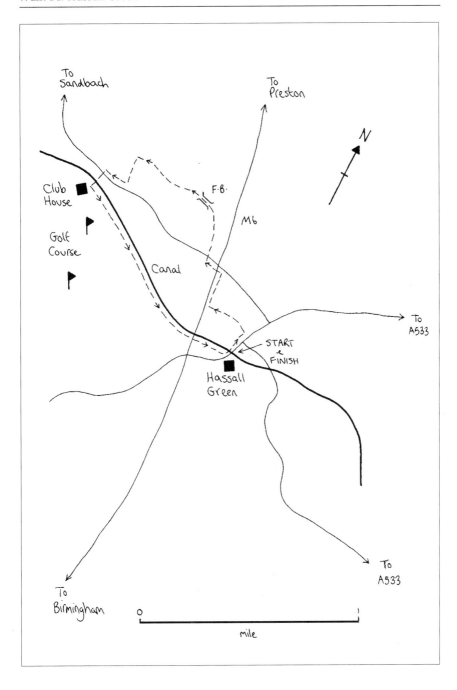

right. Stay close to the fence on your left which forms the motorway boundary. It is interesting to compare your speed with that of the traffic hurtling by. You have time to observe the landscape with its flora and fauna.

After another stile follow the same line of direction to the next before a sharp right turn brings you to Betchton Road. Turn left over the bridge spanning the motorway. Some 25 metres beyond turn right over an unsigned stile set back in the hedge and, after a mere four metres, negotiate a waymarked stile.

Cross the following field on the clearly defined path and, over the next stile which is set into a wire fence, turn left through approximately 40 degrees to an obvious waymarked stile about half way along the narrow field.

Beyond this stile continue in the same direction, still along a well-trodden path, as it skirts to the left of a wood while gradually losing height towards yet another stile after about 100 metres.

Turn right over this one, cross a wooden footbridge and, at the far side, turn sharp left as instructed by the waymark. The path now keeps to the right of a small stream as it pursues its course through a shallow valley that resembles many in the White Peak of Derbyshire, the Yorkshire Dales or the Cotswolds.

The grassland is peppered with clumps of gorse, nettle, rosebay willowherb, hawthorn, bracken and bramble while willows, oak and beech dot the gradual slopes on either side.

Stay forward over further stiles until a lane is reached. Ignore the facing stile, instead turning left as the sunken lane climbs out of the valley before regaining Betchton Road by "Woodyfields Cottage".

Turn right along the road, ignoring a footpath signed to the left, until reaching the entrance to Malkin's Bank Golf Club. Turn left into the approach road and, after only a few metres and in front of the Club House turn left onto the towpath of the Trent and Mersey canal.

Continue alongside the canal with the distinctive landmark of Mow Cop in the far distance ahead and noticing bridge number 149 which is doubled-arched to permit two way traffic.

After walking under the M6 climb slightly to a lock, turn left over the gate and then right for the Lockside Tea Room.

𝒲𝒶𝓁𝓀 15. 𝐿𝒾𝓉𝓉𝓁𝑒 𝑀𝑜𝓇𝑒𝓉𝑜𝓃 𝐻𝒶𝓁𝓁

Route: Little Moreton Hall – Boarded Barn Farm – Scholar Green – Macclesfield Canal – Old House Green – Little Moreton Hall.

Start: Car park, Little Moreton Hall. Map reference 831589

Distance: 3½ miles.

Map: "Wilmslow, Macclesfield & Congleton", no. 268 in the O.S. Explorer series.

Public Transport: None.

By Car: Little Moreton Hall is adjacent to and signed from the A34 approximately four miles south of Congleton.

The Tea Shop

The Tea Room at Little Moreton Hall is located inside the main building and, as you would expect, has black and white interior walls and wooden beams.

It serves light lunches, afternoon teas, scones where the cream is not spared, cakes, slices of home-made gateaux and fruit pies, all of which may be accompanied by a choice of speciality teas or coffee. For non National Trust members there is an admission charge to the hall.

Opening hours: April to October daily 11.30 to 5.00pm. But closed Mondays and Tuesdays except Bank Holidays. November to mid-December Saturdays and Sundays only 11.30 am to 4.00pm. Closed from mid-December to the end of March.

Little Moreton Hall

Dating from 1480 Little Moreton Hall has undergone few changes in its history so that it represents, better than perhaps any other building in England, the medieval type of architecture. Its striking black and white timber framed architecture, with its protruding gables, has made it a great favourite with photographers, both amateur and professional.

It is noted for its Long Gallery, Withdrawing Room, secret chambers, oak panelling and decorative plasterwork. Outside it is surrounded by a moat and has a very unusual Elizabethan Knot Garden. Built by the Moreton family who lived there for centuries it is now owned by the National Trust.

Opening times: March to the end of September, Wednesdays to Sun-

Little Moreton Hall

days, 12.00 a.m. to 5.30 p.m; October, Saturdays and Sundays only,
12.00 a.m. to 5.30 p.m; Closed during the winter.

The Route

From the car park entrance turn left along the A34, walking in a southerly direction and using the pavement on the western side. After 150
metres, and by a footpath finger post, turn right over a stile to walk the
path to the immediate right of a hawthorn hedge. After approximately
50 metres turn left over a stile set into that hedge and then turn right,
passing between a fence on the left and hedge on the right.

Negotiate another stile, reached after a mere 20 metres, and veer to
the right, heading for the right-hand corner of the buildings of Boarded
Barn Farm. The path actually leads to a stile and waymarkers just a few
metres to the right of a white bath.

With the farm on your left, advance to another waymarked stile
within 30 metres and adjacent to a metal five-barred gate. Over that remain to the right of a hedge to yet another waymarked stile.

Turn left and, remaining still to the right of a hedge, aim for a footpath
finger post and a small wooden gate alongside a five-barred wooden
gate. Through the gate, make a right turn along the minor road which

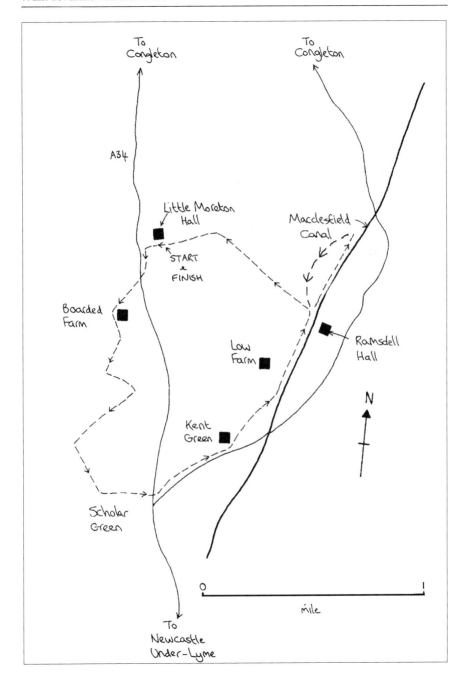

To
Congleton

To
Congleton

A34

Little Moreton
Hall

Macclesfield
Canal

START
&
FINISH

Boarded
Farm

Low
Farm

Ramsdell
Hall

N

Kent
Green

Scholar
Green

To
Newcastle
Under-Lyme

0   1

mile

eventually leads to Rode Heath. After about a quarter of a mile it dips slightly to a redbrick bridge.

At the far end of this and by a footpath sign, make a left turn over a stile and bear left, taking your line of direction from the arm of the footpath post while aiming for a gateway in the line of trees ahead.

Climb slightly, pass through the gateway to continue to the left of a row of Scots Pines. After 120 metres go through an official gap in the facing hedge and stay forward alongside a fence on your right to a stile and sign some five metres to the left of a metal five-barred gate.

On the far side turn left along a narrow lane, crossing a footbridge after 20 metres. Proceed by two houses on your left and, ignoring a signed path to your right, stay with the lane as it widens out to reach the A34 at Scholar Green.

Cross to a facing road of about 10 metres in length. At the end go left into Station Road. Initially this is lined with houses on both sides but, beyond Stone Chair Lane, open countryside replaces the houses on the left. Mow Cop is directly ahead.

By Kent Green Farm, a large and impressive redbrick house, swing left into a surfaced lane signed as a public footpath. It is a cul-de-sac leading only to Low Farm.

Where the lane dips slightly and bends round to the left on its final approach to Low Farm, go over the stile with a faded yellow waymark on your right.

Climb gently for about 150 metres to the right of a wood before gaining a stile and the towpath of the Macclesfield Canal. Turn left along the towpath which is tree lined and offers a scene of peace and tranquillity. The elevated position of the canal provides some far-reaching views out over the pastoral landscape of South Cheshire. Often, while walking this stretch, I have seen a fox scurrying over a neighbouring field even in broad daylight.

After some distance you will pass Ramsdell Hall, an imposing mansion in the classical and Jacobean styles. Its lawns, reaching down to the water's edge, are immaculate and of a quality that would put even Oval to shame.

Stay alongside the canal, going under the arched stone bridge at Old House Green and continuing with the towpath until reaching bridge number 85, another stone arched affair. Pass beneath this and immediately turn left up a flight of a dozen stone steps as directed by a yellow waymark to emerge onto New Road. Turn right along this, pass "Keeper's Cottage" on your left and lose height round a double bend.

After approximately 250 metres, and by the entrance to the driveway to Hall Farm with its cattle grid, turn left over a wooden stile adjacent to a footpath sign. Taking direction from the arm of the post, advance across the field on a fairly clear path to pass between two pylons under two sets of overhead wires. Just beyond the pylons descend the sloping field to a wooden stile set into a gap between the trees.

Maintaining the same line of direction climb the slope, stay to the left of a few solitary trees and gradually bear left while staying to the right of a belt of trees to another wooden stile by a metal 5-barred gate. Go forward across the centre of the next large field with a canal bridge a few metres to the left.

Over this stile turn right along a wide track which runs between a fence post on the left and a hedge on the right. Stay to the left of this hedge to another stile before turning sharply to the right to walk alongside a hedge which forms the boundary of a large field.

After the stile in the far corner of the field stay alongside the hedge to another and then turn through 45 degrees to the left for the crossing of the centre of another field to the diametrically opposed corner by some farm buildings.

There, negotiate another stile by a footpath sign and walk to the left of a gate, then a fence and then a hedgerow. On the far side of these is a farm house with an ancient cruck-frame barn which is as old as Little Moreton Hall and has occupied the same site for several centuries. Remarkably it remains in very good condition and is still in everyday use.

Beyond the next stile follow the broad track to pass Little Moreton Hall on your way to the car park. However, it is well worth diverting to tour this historic building and to enjoy a cream tea at the same time.

Walk 16. Marton

Route: Church Farm – Bunce Lane – Sandpit Farm – Fern Farm – Higher Gorsley Green – Davenport Lane – Oak Lane – Church Farm.

Start: Church Farm, Marton. Map reference 850681.

Distance: 4 miles.

Map: "Wilmslow, Macclesfield & Congleton", no. 268 in the O.S. Explorer series.

Public Transport: None

By Car: Marton is on the A34 between Wilmslow and Congleton, about three miles south of Monks Heath. There are minor roads to Macclesfield and Holmes Chapel.

The Tea Shop

The Farm Brasserie & Restaurant occupies two rooms, both with flagged floors, red-brick walls and thick wooden beams. The wooden furniture emphasises a rural ambience, while Tibetan carvings and a fertility window on one of the walls add an oriental flavour. Outside seating is in a landscaped garden area with pond, pergola, another fertility window and other Tibetan artefacts – owner Robert Ward has an interest in such things and also owns the Village Shop next door.

At coffee or tea time, there is a choice of home-baked cakes, gateaux, pies and tarts accompanied by a good range of teas, coffees and cold drinks. Service is efficient and attentive.

From midday (and on Friday and Saturday evenings) there is a varied selection of more substantial fare, daily items being listed on the blackboard. When last visited, these included cottage pie, pasta dishes, sauteed trout and mouthwatering desserts that included treacle tart and cherry crumble.

Opening hours: All year, Tuesday to Thursday 9am to 5pm. Friday and Saturday 9am to 11pm. Sunday 9am to 5pm. Closed Mondays. Phone 01260 224785.

Marton

Church Farm on the A34 adjacent to Marton Church has recently been developed as an arts and craft centre where it is possible to see the craftsmen in action. There is glass blowing, furniture making, painting

Marton church

craftsmen in action. There is glass blowing, furniture making, painting demonstrations and ice cream making. The Rare Breeds enclosure includes wild boar, llamas and several species of domesticated pigs.

The nearby parish church of St James and St Paul is the oldest half-timbered black and white church in Europe. Founded in 1343 as a Chantry Chapel, the oldest surviving part of the building is the nave.

The Route

After visiting the church of St James and St Paul, cross the A34 to the facing stile by the footpath finger post and maintain direction over the field aiming for the corner of a hedge approximately 100 metres ahead.

From that corner remain to the left of the hedge, passing several enormous oak trees en route to a waymarked stile in the field corner. Advance some 25 metres to a second stile which permits an exit onto Bunce Lane. Turn left for 150 metres. Beyond a Z-bend and by a metal five-barred gate and footpath sign, turn right over a stile.

Walk to the left of a fence and, subsequently, of a hedge to a facing stile and, with Bunce Lane Farm a short distance to your left, cross the middle of two successive fields to a stile by a pylon in a field corner. Using the stiles and a line of overhead wires as your guide, continue for-

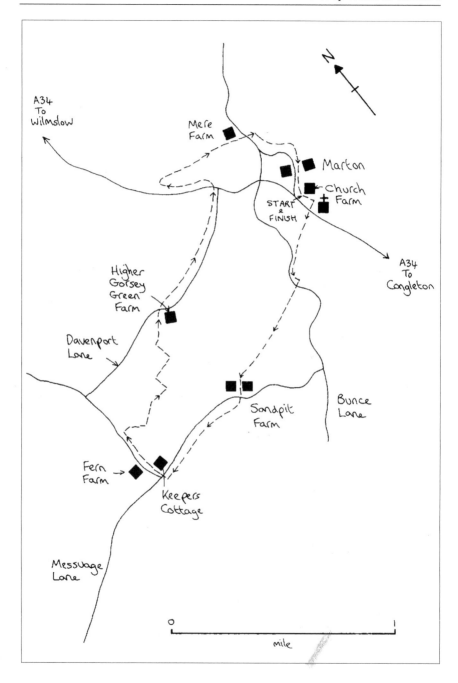

wards until passing between the house and outbuildings of Sandpit Farm which appears to specialise in the growing of garden turf.

By the house turn left along the short drive to Messuage Lane, a narrow surfaced road. Turn right and, using the wide grass verge, proceed for about half a mile.

By the far end of Keeper's Cottage, an attractive brick building, there is a T-junction. Turn right into Hodgehill Lane which is signed to Siddington Heath.

Pass Fern farm with its barking but harmless dogs and continue for about 150 metres to the entrance to Daisy Bank Farm. By the footpath sign opposite turn right through a metal five-barred gate and bear slightly to the right for an obvious stile in the facing hedgerow some 80 metres distant.

Over this stile stay close to the hedge on your right to another stile and then bear diagonally left to a fence corner as indicated by the waymarker. There turn right so that you have a fence on your immediate right. In the next field corner turn left but, after 40 metres, go right over another stile. Advance to the left of a hedge and pass to the right of a small pond to a stile which permits access to Davenport Lane.

Turn right, soon passing Higher Gorsley Green Farm with its collection of goats and continue until, by Bank Farm, you reach the A34. Cross to the pavement and turn left. After approximately 300 metres and by a footpath sign, turn right through a five-barred gate. Staying to the right of a hedge walk to the first field corner and turn left over a waymarked stile.

Immediately turn right to another stile in a wooden fence and advance to the right of the boundary of Mere Farm. By a five-barred gate turn left over another stile and turn right along the farm drive until arriving at School Lane by a footpath sign.

Turn right but at the Y-junction by the village school, fork left into Oak Lane, following this round until it reaches the 34. Turn left and pass the Davenport Arms on your right to regain Church Farm and Marton Coffee House and Brasserie.

Walk 17. Alderley Edge

Route: Alderley Edge village – Castle Rock – Armada Beacon – The Wizard – Nether Alderley Mill – Nether Alderley Church – Blackshaw Lane – Alderley Edge village.

Start: Car park, Alderley Edge village. Map reference 844783

Distance: 6½ miles

Map: "Wilmslow, Macclesfield & Congleton", no. 268 in the O.S. Explorer series.

Public Transport: Alderley Edge station is served by trains from Manchester, Stockport, Wilmslow and Crewe.

There are frequent daily (including Sunday) buses from Manchester, Wilmslow and Macclesfield.

By Car: Alderley Edge is on the A34, some three miles to the south of Wilmslow. There are two pay and display car parks in the village centre, both signed from the A34 and quite close to each other.

The Tea Shops

On this walk there is a choice of two tea shops:

The Wizard Tea Room

The Wizard Tea Room on Alderley Edge itself is a simple stone building adjoining the National Trust Information Centre. It is white both outside and in, the interior being decorated with various items of old farming equipment and horse harnesses. In winter it is heated by a blazing wood burning stove.

The menu embraces freshly cut or toasted sandwiches with a variety of fillings, soup of the day, toasted teacakes, delicious home-made scones with jam and cream and a selection of cakes, to be followed by either coffee or one of a choice of speciality teas.

Opening hours: Saturdays, Sundays and Bank Holidays 10.00am to 5.00pm; weekday groups on request. Phone: 01625 572706.

The Lemon Tree

Located on the western side of London Road, in the centre of Alderley Edge, the Lemon Tree is a combined delicatessen, brasserie and coffee shop. With its tiled floor, partially tiled walls and light colours, it offers a delightfully bright and cheerful environment. It is furnished with circular tables and modern furniture.

Throughout the day it offers a selection of speciality teas and coffees, while its fruit drinks are fresh and organic. Any of these may be accompanied by a choice from the wide range of tempting-looking scones, croissants, Danish pastries and other cakes.

For those in search of something more substantial, the Lemon Tree tempts with some most unusual dishes. For 'Starters' you could try Cheese and Roast Tomato Tart or Wild Mushroom Risotto. This could be followed by a Seafood Platter of smoked trout, smoked salmon, prawns and mussels, or a Continental Platter with its choice of cheeses. The Italian Antipasti offers a selection of cured hams and salamis, while the Best of British Platter consists of roast meats, British cheeses, cold pies and chutney. There is also a selection of exotic sandwiches.

Opening hours: All year Tuesday to Saturday 10.00am to 5.00pm. Closed Sunday and Monday. **Phone:** 01625 583858

Alderley Edge

Alderley Edge is one of several sandstone escarpments rising abruptly from the Cheshire Plain. Now owned by the National Trust, it is more than 600 feet above the surrounding countryside thereby affording some extensive views over towards Kinder Scout, Bleaklow and other outstanding features within the Peak District National Park.

Copper was first mined there by the Romans, the industry continuing at intervals until it finally ceased during the nineteenth century. The mines are now closed and sealed-off from the general public but occasional guided tours are arranged by the National Trust in association with a local caving club.

Beacon Point marks the site where a bonfire was lit on the approach of the Spanish Armada in 1588, one of many such early warning signals organised in a chain throughout England to alert the local militia to be prepared in case of an invasion.

As with other sites throughout Britain, Alderley Edge is closely linked in popular mythology with King Arthur. According to one legend the king, with all the Knights of the Round Table, sleeps in one of the great caverns awaiting the time when this country once again requires their help.

The Wizard Hotel takes its name from Merlin, who, according to another popular tale, met a drunken farmer on his way home over the

Edge and took him into the cavern to sell his horse to a knight who did not have one.

The village, which takes its name from this sandstone ridge, was once the home of the important Stanley Family, one of their number serving as Dean of Westminster. It developed during the nineteenth century into a residential area for Manchester cotton magnates and business men who built the fine houses, many of which have now been converted into flats.

Nether Alderley Mill

It is known that a mill existed in Alderley as early as 1290 but no details have survived about its exact location. The present building dates from the sixteenth century and is unusual because the rear faces the embankment of the reservoir constructed to store water for driving the machinery.

It was worked by a long line of millers until the early 1940s when extensive repairs were needed. In view of the declining trade for such mills, the cost of saving it was prohibitive and a decision was taken to close it down.

After the Second World war it was given to the National Trust and in 1967 an imaginative renovation programme was launched which resulted in its restoration to full working order. For details of opening times ring 01625 523012.

Nether Alderley Church

This is a fourteenth century building with a broad, low tower. Inside there is an unusual pew which resembles a box at a theatre. This is the Stanley family pew decorated with the coats-of-arms of several important families to whom they are related. Their residence was Nether Alderley Hall which still stands on the opposite side of the A34.

The Route

From either of the two car parks turn right along London Road. By the major and complicated traffic junction opposite the Trafford Arms, make an acute left turn into Chapel Road, continuing along it as it becomes Mottram Road. Just beyond the cricket ground on your left swing right into "Squirrel's Jump".

This rough lane climbs for some 250 metres to a through stile which affords access to National Trust property. Stay with the broad track as it ascends for a further 100 metres before levelling out to contour the north face of the Edge.

Bridleway at Alderley Edge

After several hundred metres through magnificent beech and other deciduous trees a flight of wooden steps is reached. Turn right up these for a steep climb which arcs round to the left by several outcrops of red sandstone rock.

A short distance beyond where these terminate make a right turn up a shorter flight of steps and pass through two stone gateposts before making a left turn onto a large slab of rock which is known as "Castle Rock". This provides a panoramic view over the Cheshire Plain and Mersey Valley as far as the West Pennine Moors north of Bolton, recognised by the TV masts on Winter Hill. To the east the dominant peat plateaux of Kinder Scout and Bleaklow are two distinctive landmarks within the Peak District National Park.

From Castle Rock continue along the Edge, staying just to the left of a wire fence until reaching a stone wall on your right. By the corner of this turn right, taking any of the plethora of paths leading up to Beacon point, commemorated by a plaque set into a stone plinth.

Stay to the left of the Beacon, heading for a clear, well-maintained path identified by a wheelchair sign. At the next cross-roads in the path network continue straight ahead to the right of a very large patch of sandy ground running into a small valley.

This is where some of the former mines are located, so extreme care should be taken to avoid it. Maintain your direction along the path until emerging through a wooden stile onto a very broad path by the Wizard Tea Rooms and the National Trust Information Centre. Turn left, pass to the right of "Forester's Lodge" but, after 200 metres and just beyond a bend, make a right turn over a stile to walk between two wire fences.

Over the stile at the bottom of the dip climb to Edge House Farm, cross a broad track to another stile and lose height for a short distance down a field before turning right over another stile.

The path once again passes between wire fences but, after 50 metres and yet another stile, turns sharply to the left along a much broader track with a hedgerow on the left and a fence on the right.

At the foot of the gentle slope negotiate a stile but maintain your direction to the next stile where the waymarks offer a choice of three alternative routes.

Turn sharp right along the edge of a field and, after another stile, continue forward along a surfaced drive leading to Hill Top Farm which is a short distance off your route to the left.

100 metres beyond a cattle grid make a right turn over a stile to cross one field to Adders Moss Farm. Climb the stile alongside the garage, cross the driveway directly to another stile, walk just to the left of a hedge along the front of the house and turn right, as indicated by a waymarker arrow, before making a left turn over a stile.

Keep to the extreme right of a small paddock, climb a stile, continue forward to a large gate and pass a house on the left before reaching the B5087, the Alderley Edge to Macclesfield road.

Cross directly to the signed path running through Finlow Hill Wood. Where this short stretch ends turn right along a narrow surfaced road, passing a set of riding stables on your left. After a few hundred metres, follow the road round to the right but, where it swings right for a second time, continue directly ahead into Bradford Lane with its rough surface.

Stay with Bradford Lane to pass Bradford Lodge Nurseries and the Wizard Caravan Park until, a short distance beyond Bradford Lodge Farm, it acquires a cobbled surface.

By "The Spinney" Bradford Lane is joined from the left by Hocker Lane. Keep forward to reach the A34, the main trunk road joining Manchester with Congleton, Birmingham and Southampton.

Turn left for the short distance to Alderley Mill which is on your left. A few metres beyond this ancient monument make a right turn into the narrow road signed to Nether Alderley Church.

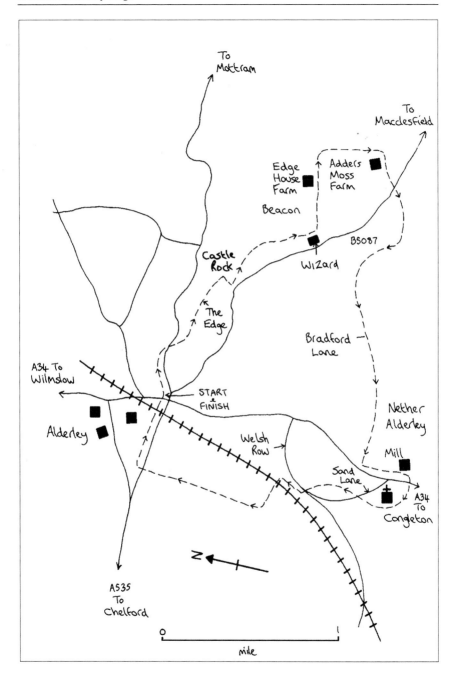

Continue into the churchyard, passing to the right of the tiny school, constructed of local sandstone in 1628 at the expense of Hugh Shaw Clark, and the Mausoleum which houses the remains of former members of the Stanley family.

Keep to the left of the church itself to reach a stone stile in the facing wall. This has a small flight of steps leading down into the churchyard extension. Cross this to a wooden stile and maintain direction to a footpath finger post with five arms erected by the Peak and Northern Footpath Society alongside another stile. Negotiate this and continue the same line across a large field following the footpath signed to "Chorley via Walton Farm".

Head for the stile in the facing hawthorn hedge. Cross directly over Sand Lane to a footpath finger post and keep to the footpath sandwiched between a hedge to the left and a fence to the right and flanked by houses on both sides.

After 100 metres pass beneath a giant oak and cross a wooden footbridge with stiles at either end before veering very slightly to the left, as directed by the footpath sign, while aiming for a gap in the line of trees ahead.

Through that gap stay forward through an intermittent line of trees before heading for the left-hand corner of the boundary hedge surrounding a redbrick house. There you will encounter a footpath sign with a stile adjacent.

This provides an exit onto Welsh Row, a narrow, surfaced road. Turn right for some 400 metres. Opposite a house, "Tara", turn left through a holly hedge onto a path recognised by an obscured footpath sign.

The path keeps to the right of another hedge and to the left of a fence to a stile within 100 metres. Over this continue to the left of a fence. On gaining the first field corner make a right turn over a stile and, now with a wire fence on your left, walk along the field boundary until reaching a wooden five-barred gate, also on your left.

Turn left over the adjacent stile, again partially obscured by an overgrown holly tree. From this point onwards the path develops into a lane, lined on both sides by large trees. It crosses above the main Manchester to Crewe railway line by a bridge.

At the far end of this turn right through a hedge, the gap having a footpath sign but no stile or gate. Keep to this broad track with the railway moving further away to the right and the tall, conspicuous steeple of Alderley Edge Church visible in the far distance ahead.

Over the next stile cross the field corner, as instructed by a waymark, and continue to the left of the meandering field boundary. Ignore an isolated wooden stile on your right, continuing for a further 250 metres to a facing stile alongside a five-barred gate.

Over that turn right along Blackshaw Lane which is flanked by hedges until meeting a Y-junction. Fork right, the lane now acquiring a surface and houses on both sides until it meets the road from Alderley Edge to Chorley. Again turn right, using great caution in the absence of a pavement, to cross back over the railway to the village centre by the Trafford Arms on the A34. Turn left for the car park.

Walk 18. Prestbury

Route: Prestbury – Spittle House – Woodend Farm – Legh hall – Mottram Wood – Bollin Valley – Prestbury.

Start: New Road, Prestbury, outside the White House restaurant. Map reference 900769

Distance: 4 miles.

Map: "Wilmslow, Macclesfield & Congleton", no. 268 in the O.S. Explorer series.

Public Transport: Prestbury station is served by frequent daily (including Sunday) trains from Manchester, Stockport, Macclesfield and Stoke-on-Trent. Prestbury is also served by frequent buses from Macclesfield and Wilmslow (Monday to Friday).

By Car: Prestbury is about three miles north of Macclesfield and may be reached by either of two minor roads from the A523 or the A538 from Wilmslow. There are two large free car parks in the village.

The Tea Shops

Despite the popularity of the village, there is no tea shop as such in Prestbury. There is an abundance of restaurants for more substantial meals but seemingly nowhere for more modest refreshment.

Fortunately for walkers, however, there is The Bridge Hotel which has become a popular meeting place for both locals and visitors. This was once a row of timbered cottages dating from 1626. In 1745, one of the cottages provided lodging for Bonnie Prince Charlie as he travelled south with his Scottish army. In 1952, the row of cottages was acquired and developed into the hotel and restaurant that we see today.

In the hotel lounge you can select from a choice of pastries, scones, flapjacks and other goodies, accompanied by coffee in various styles, hot chocolate or a choice of teas. If it so happens that you complete your walk by lunchtime, the restaurant offers an excellent and well-priced luncheon (in 2005, £9.50 for two courses, £12.50 for three courses).

Open every day of the week, all year. Phone 01625 829326.

Prestbury

The name "Prestbury" is derived from "Priests' Burgh" and is indicative of a very early Christian foundation with a group of clergy serving a very

The Bridge Hotel

wide area. As proof of this there is a fragment of an Anglo-Saxon stone cross, discovered during the nineteenth century and now preserved in a glass case in the churchyard.

Also in the churchyard is a Norman chapel which was rebuilt during the eighteenth century. Much of the present church dates from the thirteenth century with later additions and alterations and includes memorials to several local families.

Another reminder of Prestbury's medieval history is the Spittle House. Today it is a private residence

The 1448 Priest's House – now a bank

but originally, as its name implies, it was a hospital run by the church authorities.

The village itself is a mixture of architectural styles from medieval black and white half-timbered houses through Georgian to nineteenth century weavers' cottages. The Priest's House, built in 1448, remains in use as a bank and the large white house at the southern end of the main street is Prestbury Hall.

The Route

From the start point close to the junction of Macclesfield Road and Wilmslow Road in the centre of Prestbury, turn right along New Road, to pass Prestbury church.

Cross the stone bridge over the River Bollin, here flowing over a cobbled bed, and turn left into Bollin Grove which is signed as part of the Bollin Way to Wilmslow.

The Bollin Valley Way runs for 30 miles from the Macclesfield Riverside Park to the Manchester Ship Canal along the banks of the River Bollin. It was established under the auspices of the Bollin Valley Project, an experimental pilot scheme launched by the Countryside Commission in 1973 to develop open-air recreation in the countryside along the urban fringes.

The river is now on your left but look out for the colourful garden of "Riverside Cottage" on your right, a short distance before passing the Methodist Church.

Bollin Grove continues beyond the village school and a row of old redbrick cottages intermingled with more substantial modern residences. Where Bollin Grove ends, with a playing field on your left and another Bollin Valley way sign on your right, maintain direction along a broad chatter track.

On approaching a concrete bridge with white railings, ignore a stile on your right and yet another sign pointing towards Wilmslow. Instead, go left over the Bollin with the track. A short distance in front of Spittle House, go left over a stile to follow a field path as it runs to the left of a hedge of copper beech to another stile.

Continue close to the hedge and then, in the far corner of the field, turn right over a stile, advancing about 30 metres to a waymarker post. There, turn left down a flight of steps, climb another stile, negotiate a footbridge over the stream and climb five wooden steps. At the head of these swing left, aiming for a stile in the corner of the field.

Over that advance a further 10 metres to a second stile and then walk

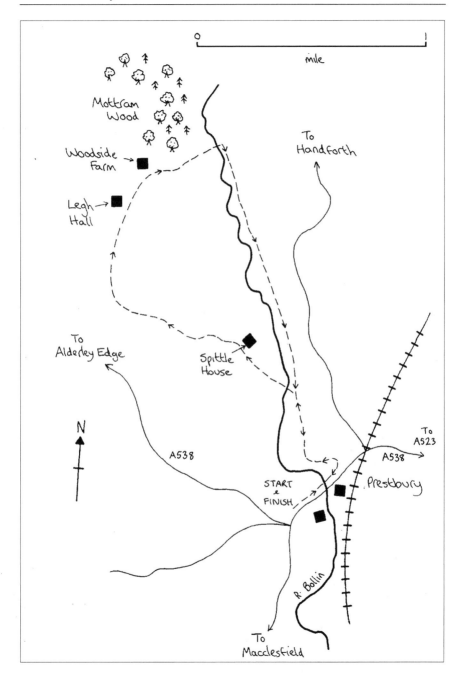

a little to the right of a wire fence. Half way along the field boundary and by a metal five-barred gate, turn left over a stile to pass a small coppice of trees planted by the Bollin Valley Project.

Keeping the fence on your right, continue to the corner of the field before reaching a stile on the right which provides access to a broad lane. Turn left along this but, where it ends, cross the driveway leading to Woodend Farm, climb the obvious stile and follow the path signed to Mottram St Andrew as it crosses the field.

Stay forward to a solitary chestnut tree, lose altitude slightly to a wooden footbridge over a marshy area and maintain the same line of direction towards the right-hand corner of another coppice.

Advance with this on your left but, by the far corner, swing sharply to the left and head for a waymarker post while staying to the right of a line of hawthorn trees. Over the next stile continue with a ditch and fence on your left, ignoring a sign showing a path off to the left towards Prestbury Road.

Negotiate another stile and partner the hedge on your left while proceeding round the corner of the field to another footpath sign. Directed by this, turn left through a metal kissing gate onto a broad track, soon reaching a junction in the network of lanes by Legh Hall.

Turn right by the footpath signpost, walking by the side of Legh Hall itself to another kissing gate. Through this, traverse the long meadow in a straight line, climb a stile on the left and, maintaining the same general line of direction, keep forward to Woodside Farm.

Cross the driveway directly, negotiate a stile and then turn sharp right to pass alongside the barn and a spasmodic row of trees to another stile which provides access to Mottram Wood.

The path through this is clear and easy to follow until it emerges into a large grass paddock surrounded on all sides by mature deciduous trees. This spot is rural Cheshire at its finest.

Cross the paddock in a straight line, climb a stile, turn right as directed by a footpath sign and descend to a footbridge spanning the River Bollin. On the far bank turn right along the riverside path, staying with it beyond the Water Treatment Works until it emerges onto Bollin Grove. Retrace your steps to the start point.

Walk 19. Kettleshulme

Route: Kettleshulme – Taxal Edge – Windgather Rocks – Pym Chair – Jenkin Chapel – Summer Close – Kettleshulme.

Start: The junction of Paddock Lane and the B5470 in the centre of Kettleshulme village. Map reference 987796.

Alternative start: Pym Chair car park. Map reference 995768. From Kettleshulme follow signs towards Goyt Valley and the car park is located by the T-junction beyond Windgather Rocks.

Distance: 7 miles.

Map: "The Peak District: White Peak Area", No. 24 in the O.S. "Outdoor Leisure" series.

Public Transport: Kettleshulme is served by daily (including Sunday) bus service from Macclesfield and Whaley Bridge.

By Car: Kettleshulme is on the B5470 between Macclesfield and Whaley Bridge. There is limited parking in Paddock Lane.

The Tea Shop

Dunge Valley Gardens in the Todd Brook Valley beneath Windgather Rocks were initiated several years ago by David Ketley and his wife, Elizabeth, to grow shrubs and plants normally associated with high altitudes. Many of the species have been reared from seeds collected by David in the Himalayas and one of the specialties is the numerous varieties of Rhododendron.

With more and more visitors a tea room has been opened. Walkers are welcome except on busy Sundays and Bank Holidays. Patrons in either the café or seated outside on the patio may enjoy views over the surrounding countryside and, closer to hand, the gardens which David and Elizabeth have created.

In addition to a range of home-made cakes and gateaux Elizabeth serves light meals such as Quiche Lorraine, soup with roll and a selection of sandwiches, all accompanied by a choice of tea, coffee or soft drink.

Opening hours: currently 10.30am to 5.00pm, Thursday to Sunday, March and April; Tuesday to Sunday in May; Thursday to Sunday, June to August. Closed for the rest of the year.

The Route

From its junction with Paddock Lane, walk along the B5470 in the direction of Macclesfield but, after less than 100 metres and by the far corner of St James's School, turn left into the very narrow Side End Lane. After a further 100 metres turn left by a footpath sign into a lane which passes to the left of two bungalows.

By the end of the second, "Ash Tree", negotiate a stone step stile to the left of a metal five-barred gate and stay forward while veering slightly to the right to reach the end corner of a collapsed wall. From there stay to the right of the foundations to a stile in a facing wall and then proceed to the right of a wall to a stone step stile.

Over this turn right along a lane, following it for a short distance as it corners left around a stone cottage. By the far end of the cottage pass through a five-barred metal gate to stay with the track as it runs to the right of a wall which forms the field boundary.

Half way along the field the track swings right towards a farm. At this point stay forward by leaving the track and taking a narrow path which clings to a wall on the left as it heads towards a stone step stile.

Over this keep to the left of the farm as the path dips, crosses a narrow stream by means of a single stepping stone, and reaches a stile. From there the clear, distinct path climbs alongside a line of wooden telegraph poles carrying overhead wires, while staying to the left of a large expanse of gorse.

Eventually the path levels to go between two stone gateposts, crosses another stream and continues to the right of a hedge composed almost entirely of hawthorn and holly. After a short distance it resumes its upward course to a Y-junction by the end of the gorse patch. Fork right to a wall corner before staying to the right of a drystone wall for some 25 metres until reaching a telegraph pole. At this point swing right again to a stile at the junction of a minor moorland road with the driveway leading to Clough Farm.

Turn left along the road. 100 metres beyond a pebble-dashed cottage on your right, by a broken footpath sign and opposite the entrance to the driveway to Wright's Farm, turn right over a stone step stile.

Climb the centre of the field until reaching the end of a derelict wall. Stay to the right of this but, where it terminates, go right towards a very conspicuous ladder stile and then stay forwards for five metres to an intersection in the path network.

Turn right and, keeping to the left of a stone wall, reach a small wooden gate after 20 metres. Through this maintain direction as the

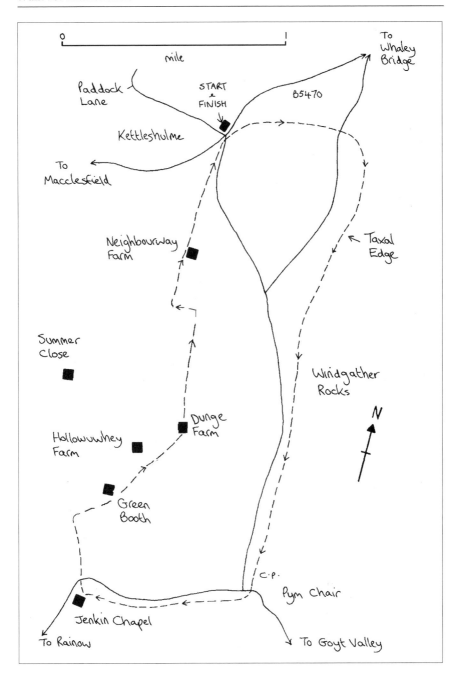

path traverses Taxal Moor onto Taxal Edge while reaching a height of 370 metres above sea level. You are actually walking along the boundary between Cheshire and Derbyshire.

To the right the village of Kettleshulme nestles in the valley of the Todd Brook with another ridge, formed by the Bowstones, Charles Head and the Blue Boar, acting as a backdrop.

To the east there are glimpses of Kinder Scout and the Colborne Moors in the Peak District National Park. After passing a short distance to the left of a farm ignore a prominent yellow arrow fixed to a tree and pointing leftwards. Instead stay forward, still keeping to the left of a drystone wall to reach the corner of a conifer plantation, the Goyt Forest.

Now actually inside Derbyshire, advance to the left of the boundary wall of the plantation and, beyond a tall ladder stile spanning a wire fence, maintain direction for a further 250 metres before the path, still between a wall on the right and a fence on the left, corners right through 90 degrees. Still climbing gradually, it reaches another tall ladder stile.

On the far side turn left along the edge of Windgather Rocks to enjoy an excellent all-round panorama of rolling moorlands with several prominent landmarks to pin-point.

Soon the path approaches close to the minor road linking Kettleshulme with the Goyt Valley. However, do not go onto the road. Climb a ladder stile to walk the concessionary footpath which runs parallel for almost a mile until it passes through the car park at Pym Chair to emerge onto a road junction.

Turn right along the road signed to Rainow, losing altitude rapidly as it corkscrews down to the Todd Brook Valley and reaches Jenkin Chapel. This eighteenth-century church, built to resemble a house, stands at what was once an important junction of packhorse routes. Controversy surrounds the origin of the name but it is probable that it derives from a fiery Welsh preacher who once addressed the cattle dealers at the horse fairs held there.

At the junction by the chapel, the road to Rainow bends round sharply to the left as it corners the chapel. Leave this road by staying forward a few metres to a Peak and Northern Footpath Society sign indicating a route to Kettleshulme.

By this, turn right over a stone step stile and veer left by a few degrees to a waymarked wooden five-barred gate. Pass through this and continue on a leftwards course until reaching a chatter track.

Turn right along this to pass to the left of the derelict Crabtree Farm. At the junction go right to follow the signed path to Green Booth. There

Jenkin Chapel, near Kettleshulme

corner the buildings leftwards before curving to the right round the base of a small knoll and crossing a stream to negotiate a stile. Immediately beyond this fork right and, keeping a stone wall on your immediate left, proceed to yet another stile.

Over this remain alongside the wall for a short distance before veering right across the field to a facing stile and then crossing the end of the subsequent small field to another stile . Cross the infant Todd Brook and take a well-earned rest at the Dunge Valley tea shop.

Suitably refreshed take the main track down the valley as it negotiates Dunge Clough before eventually acquiring a hard surface. After a further quarter of a mile, and by Five-Lane-Ends, turn left along a path running to the left of a wall, staying with it until reaching Near Carr Farm. Turn right along a lane to pass through the yard of Neighbourway Farm and by a cottage on the right with a carved plaque over the door bearing the inscription,

"G.B.
1752"

Beyond this, the track emerges onto Side End Lane just outside the village of Kettleshulme. Turn left for the final 100 metres to the B5470 and then right to your starting point.

Walk 20. Wildboarclough

Route: Brookside – Clough Brook – Lower House Cottage – Allgreave – Burntcliffe Top – Heild End – Berry Bank – Brookside.

Start: The lay-by near Brookside Restaurant. Map reference 980681

Distance: 4¼ miles.

Map: "The Peak District; White Peak Area", No. 24 in the O.S. "Outdoor Leisure" series.

Public Transport: Restricted bus service from Macclesfield.

By Car: Wildboarclough is reached by a minor road signed from the A537, Macclesfield to Buxton road and the A54, Buxton to Congleton road.

The Tea Shop

As the name implies the Brookside Restaurant is delightfully situated alongside Clough Brook in the very heart of Wildboarclough, one of Cheshire's most popular walking areas. The ancient millstone grit cottage, painted white, nestles under Shuttlingsloe, its external antiquity matched internally by thick oak beams and pillars. The white, stone walls are decorated with horns, bugles and deer's heads while tiny niches house model horses. There is nothing old-fashioned about the menu which ranges from full meals of steak and kidney pie and mixed grills, all home-made, to light snacks, sandwiches, salads, scones with jam and cream, gateaux and full afternoon teas. As befits a café long associated with the great outdoors the pots of tea are generous.

Opening hours: Saturday and Sunday all year, 12 noon to 5.00pm; phone: 01260 227632.

Wildboarclough

Regarded by many people as one of the most attractive valleys in the Peak District National Park, Wildboarclough lies entirely within the county of Cheshire. Although popular with visitors at week-ends, the crowds are soon left behind by those walking the abundance of footpaths radiating out from this dramatic moorland valley.

The last wild boar, the animal which obviously gave its name to the clough, was hunted to extinction during the fifteenth century. Although now difficult to imagine, the valley was home to three water-powered silk mills during the eighteenth century when the canal pioneer, James Brindley, installed some of the machinery. In later years the mills turned to the production of carpets, some of which were featured in the Great Exhibition of 1851. The last of the mills was demolished in 1958. Much of the land in the area is owned by the Earl of Derby who used Crag Hall as one of his country seats.

Within the last few years a freak thunderstorm and cloud-burst over the moorlands surrounding the "Cat and Fiddle" at the head of the valley created a flash flood which rushed down the bed of Clough Brook and tributary streams. One person died: roads, bridges, cars, trees and drystone walls were swept away. Many footpaths were obliterated.

A quick response by Cheshire County Council, aided by the Countryside Commission, Macclesfield Borough Council, the Peak District National Park and other bodies resulted in speedy restoration, albeit at enormous cost. One benefit has been the renewal of footbridges, footpaths and footpath signs.

The Route

From the southern end of the small lay-by and by the footpath finger post, turn left into the driveway to the Brookside Restaurant. Cross the bridge spanning Clough Brook and, immediately, turn right as directed

Crag Hall

by the waymarker to cross the patch of greensward before walking to the left of the brook and by a line of fir trees.

Undoubtedly the peace and tranquillity will be shattered by the raucous calls of the mallard which appear to inhabit this stretch of the water permanently. After 100 metres negotiate a stile but maintain the line of direction by traversing the bottom of a field which slopes upwards to your left and with a wire fence separating you from Clough Brook on your right.

Beyond the next waymarked stile climb slightly above the stream until meeting a stone wall. Keep to the left of this as it curves a few metres to a footpath sign and then keep forward, still to the left of the wall, until reaching a stone step stile adjacent to a wooden five-barred gate. Advance to the left of a barn and cottage into a walled lane which curves to the left while offering a charming view of the lower valley with its lush green hills checkered by drystone walls. On your immediate left is a wood but this terminates by the first cattle-grid. Pass to the left of some derelict farm buildings while ignoring a path to the right signed to "Wildboarclough and Owler's Bridge", instead negotiating another stile alongside the second cattle-grid. All the time the valley widens out and the wide lane makes for some excellent walking.

Beyond a third cattle-grid the lane climbs gradually between verges producing primroses, foxgloves, ivy and bramble in due season. Finally it emerges onto the A54, the Congleton to Buxton road. Turn right for the 100 metres to the "Rose and Crown" at Allgreave. By the far corner of the pub fork left into the minor moorland road signed to Quarnford, for a gradual climb with the Dane Valley and Bach Forest away to your right.

Pass Midgeley Farm first and then Pearls Farm as the view expands to include the Roaches, the famous Staffordshire rock formation which, from this angle, assumes a very dramatic aspect.

After approximately one mile the "Eagle and Child" is reached at Burntcliffe Top. This sturdy upland house boasts a plaque bearing the outline of an eagle carrying a child with the inscription:

H
17 JS 38

This is the sign of the old pub which was constructed at this spot in 1738 to serve refreshments to weary travellers using the old packhorse routes from Wildboarclough to Gradbach Mill in the nearby Dane Valley and from Three Shires Heads to Allgreave. The latter has now been surfaced for use by cars. After it ceased trading as a pub the "Eagle and

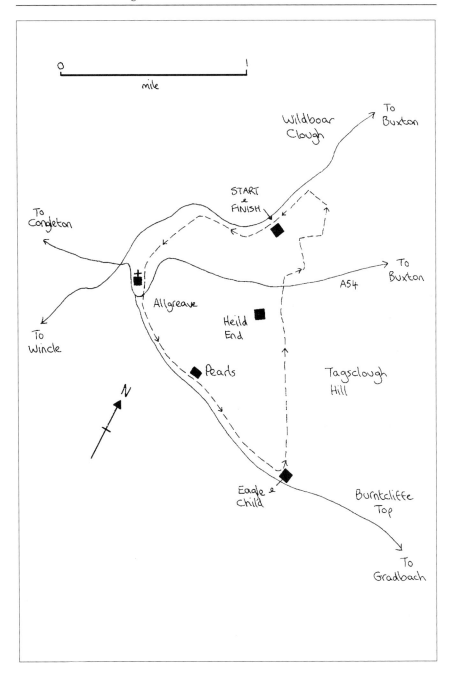

Child" was converted into a cafe, well-patronised by both walkers and cyclists. Sadly, for a variety of reasons, it has been converted into a private dwelling house.

By the far corner of the "Eagle and Child" make a sharp left turn into the unsigned bridleway which climbs steeply in the form of a walled lane for a short distance to reach a five-barred metal gate with a Peak District National Park notice alongside requesting the closure of all gates because of grazing stock. Beyond this gate the rough track stays to the left of a wall but soon becomes open on both sides as it traverses a landscape rather reminiscent of Scottish Border country with its rounded, grassy slopes.

Pass through a succession of gates until crossing a small, heather-covered plateau to the left of Tagsclough Hill before descending steeply with the summit of Shuttlingsloe on the far side of Wildboarclough directly ahead. The bridleway corkscrews down the hillside until forming a junction with the approach drive to Heild End Farm, from where it tumbles down the slope to meet the A54. Turn right along this road for approximately 100 metres to a footpath sign where a left turn over a stile provides access to a footpath crossing an upland pasture.

Aim for the very low drystone wall on your right and then, directed by a series of waymarks, stay to the left of it and also of an old stone barn. By the far end of this turn left through a gateway before swinging right through 45 degrees towards a gap in the wall.

Through this veer left towards the corner of a fir plantation where another swing further towards the left leads to a stone step stile. Turn right for the descent of a very muddy track between stone walls to a waymarker post. This offers two choices. Opt for the left-hand path across the corner of a field towards a waymarker post in front of a line of trees.

Maintain the same line of direction to a wall corner before crossing a stream and making a sharp turn to the left and staying between two walls while advancing to yet another waymarker post, again offering two choices. Continue to the right of the wall to a stile and then turn right through a small wood for approximately 20 metres. Veer left down a steep slope through the trees to a wooden footbridge spanning Clough Brook. At the far end negotiate a squeezer stile onto the road through Wildboarclough and turn left for the final few metres to the Brookside Restaurant and the car.

Walk 21. Lyme Park

Route: Lyme Hall – Crow Wood – Elmerhurst Cottage – Cockhead Farm – Bollinhurst Bridge – East Lodge – Lyme Hall.

Start: The main car park, Lyme Park, Disley. Map reference 963824. An alternative start may be made from the main entrance on the A6.

Distance: 4½ miles.

Map: "The Peak District, Dark Peak Area", no. 1 in the O.S. Outdoor Leisure series.

Public Transport: The main entrance to Lyme Park on the A6 north of Disley is served by frequent daily (including Sunday) buses from Manchester, Stockport, Buxton, Bakewell, Matlock, Derby and Nottingham. There are frequent daily (including Sunday) trains from Manchester, Stockport and Buxton to Disley station, about half a mile from the main entrance.

By Car: The main entrance to Lyme Park is on the A6, a few miles south of Stockport and about half a mile north of Disley. The main car park is approximately one mile inside the park from the entrance.

The Tea Shops

The former Lakeside Café is now known as the Park Coffee shop. It is located in the same building, a large, airy brick affair overlooking the lake close to the car park. The interior has white painted walls, wooden block floors and large wooden roof beams.

The menu, which is extensive, includes soup of the day with roll, jacket potatoes with such varied fillings as cheese, baked beans, tuna or coleslaw. There are salads with ham, cheese, turkey or chicken and a selection of sandwiches or filled rolls. The home-made cakes vary daily but usually include such favourites as flapjack, carrot cake, Victoria Sponge and chocolate fudge. There is a separate children's menu. All may be accompanied by a choice of speciality teas and coffees or soft drinks.

Opening hours: April to the end of October, daily from 11am to 5pm. November to March, Saturdays and Sundays only, 11am to 4 pm. December 27th to January 1st, daily 11pm to 4pm. Phone: 01663 766 492. The more formal Tea Room in the former Servants' Hall offers a similar menu and is open daily only from Easter to the end of October from 11am to 5pm. Closed Thursdays and Fridays. Phone, as above.

Lyme Hall

The home of the Legh family for more than 600 years, Lyme Hall contains interiors from various periods of history including Elizabethan, Stuart, Georgian and Edwardian. The present house is a splendid example of eighteenth century Palladian architecture by the Italian Giacomo Leoni which was altered a century later by Lewis Wyatt. The contents include furniture from various periods, numerous family portraits and an outstanding collection of English clocks.

Mary Queen of Scots visited Lyme while staying at Buxton as a prisoner of Queen Elizabeth I and guarded by the Earl of Shrewsbury.

The gardens extend over more than 16 acres and include formal parterres, herbaceous borders, a Victorian conservatory and an Edwardian rose garden. The setting is a vast moorland park of 1,300 acres which is home to herds of red and fallow deer.

Lyme Cage is the square tower some distance from the hall. Built as an observation tower for watching the progress of the hunt, it was later used as a lock-up for poachers.

The Route

Exit the car park by the kiosk and make a left turn along the surfaced drive, passing to the left of the small lake. Follow this drive around the exterior of the car park as it swings round to the right for a very short climb. At the top of the rise fork right onto an unsurfaced track at the first Y-junction. After a further 120 metres, and by a wall corner, a second Y-junction is reached.

Fork right again, advancing along another rough track which accompanies a stone wall on your right while directly ahead is a wide view over Greater Manchester. As the track begins to lose height, negotiate a stile adjacent to two five-barred gates and stay forward but, 15 metres beyond, turn right over a ladder stile to take the path alongside the drystone wall forming the field boundary.

The reward at this stage is a view of the western fringes of the Peak District hills of Bleaklow and Kinder Scout. Below, but closer to hand on the left, is Platt Wood Farm.

Negotiate a wooden stile alongside a five-barred gate and, on the immediate right, a stone field barn with a rusty corrugated metal roof. Continue close to the wall and over a stone step stile in the field corner to advance to the left of Crow Wood.

Descend briefly but somewhat steeply onto a wide track that forms the approach to Platt Wood Farm, now but a short distance to your left.

Lyme Cage

Cross directly to the left of the cattle grid and proceed through a five-barred metal gate before following the path over a large field.

Veer gradually away from the wall on your left as you climb, initially aiming for a clump of trees. However, on the crown of the rise, swing leftwards to pass about midway between the trees, now on your right, and the wall on your left.

Make a line towards a clearly visible five-barred gate in the distant fence ahead. On reaching this you will find a stile some 15 metres to the right. Negotiate this before striking out over the next field while aiming for the far right-hand corner. The path, having passed between an oak tree on the left and a zinc water trough on the right, eventually meets a wide track in front of a facing drystone wall.

Turn right and pass to the left of "Elmerhurst Cottage" before negotiating a very small wooden gate followed, within 20 metres, by a large white metal one adorned with wooden fencing. Continue over two small bridges and by "Brookside Cottages" before meeting the main driveway into the park, a few metres to the right of the entrance from the A6.

Cross the drive to the left of the wooden kiosk but, by the first corner of "Red Lane Cottage", turn left through a tall wooden gate onto a lane which passes to the right of some boarding kennels and the complex belonging to the North West Water PLC.

Leaving these behind continue along the lane. Ignore a footpath signed off to the left after 350 metres, climbing more steeply for a further 100 metres.

By the first corner of the first house and by another footpath sign, turn right over a wooden stile. Keep to the right of a stone wall with a lapwood fence on top and parallel with some overhead wires.

Over the stile in the field corner, turn left through ninety degrees to pass to the right of a private tennis court and a row of holly and hawthorn trees until arriving at the surfaced approach lane to Bollinhurst Reservoir. Turn right along this for a quarter of a mile. By the derelict Cockhead Farm and before a set of double wooden gates turn left to negotiate an unsigned stile adjacent to a metal five-barred gate.

Do not go through these wooden gates because the path beyond leads to the reservoir enclosure which is forbidden to the public. Instead, remain to the left of a wire fence until the first field corner. There swing left to a rather large telegraph pole before veering to the right and staying to the left of a drystone wall. This wall separates you from Bollinhurst Reservoir while Horse Coppice Reservoir is behind you.

Over a stone step stile in the next wall corner continue alongside the wall until, beyond the head of Bollinhurst Reservoir, the path swings left to enter some woods by a strange and unusual stile which has three uprights.

Having negotiated this, swing slightly to the left, traverse a low ridge between two streams and emerge into a very green pasture. Follow the clear path across the greensward until it reaches a bridleway by a Peak and Northern Footpath Society sign adjacent to a stile.

Ignore a facing path signed to Kettleshulme and turn right along the sunken lane which is lined with oak, holly, sycamore and bramble, not to mention foxglove. Lose height before crossing Bollinhurst Bridge and climbing steeply to re-enter Lyme Park by the gate at East Lodge.

The track traverses high ground so affording some views of the surrounding moorlands. Lyme Cage eventually appears to your right with red deer grazing all around it. The going is easy and relaxed. Continue until the track acquires a surface and loses height to pass in front of Lyme Hall. If you desire the Tea Rooms turn left through the Hall entrance. Otherwise, continue forward down a long flight of steps leading to both the new Lakeside Coffee Shop and the car park.

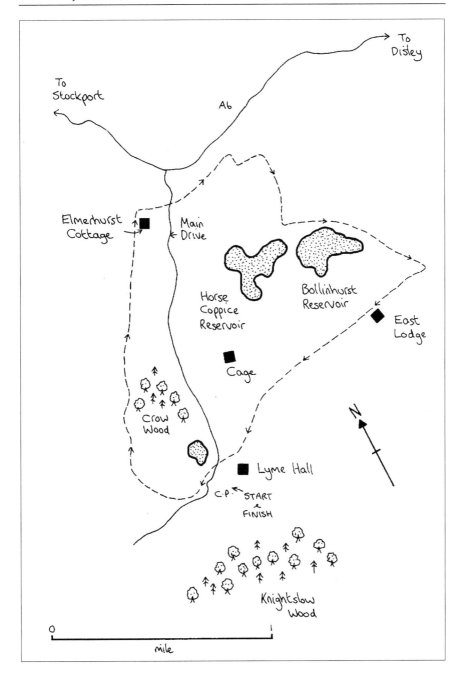

Walk 22. Pott Shrigley

Route: Coffee Tavern – Moorside Lane – Keeper's Cottage – Sponds Hill –
Bowstonegate – Knightslow Wood – Coffee Tavern

Start: The Coffee Tavern near Pott Shrigley. Map reference 944803

Distance: 5 miles.

Map: "Wilmslow, Macclesfield & Congleton", no. 268 in the O.S. Explorer series.

Public Transport: None.

By Car: The Coffee Tavern is situated on the minor road from Pott Shrigley
to Higher Poynton and is signed from Norman's Hall Farm (Map reference
936801). Roadside parking. Please do not leave your car in the Tavern's car
park because other patrons may wish to park while you are absent.

The Coffee Tavern

Unusually the Coffee Tavern is constructed of corrugated metal sheeting. It was built in 1897 as a Public Reading Room and Library by Miss
Eleanor Constance Lowther, a member of the local landed family, to
mark the Diamond Jubilee of Queen Victoria. It was also used for
church services and for social gatherings for the local inhabitants. After
ceasing to fulfil its original function between the two World Wars it was
converted to the Coffee Tavern and Tea Rooms.

In those days it was extremely popular with ramblers from the Manchester and Stockport areas. After the Second World War trade declined and it was converted into a storage depot by a local plumber. It
was eventually re-opened as the Coffee Tavern by its owner at the suggestion of his son, Andrew Buffey, a trained chef who is now in charge
of all the cooking.

It serves snacks and full meals throughout the day and is renowned
for its home-baked scones, cream gateaux, cakes and other delicacies,
one of the most popular dishes being Sticky Toffee Pudding. These are
all washed down with an admirable choice of coffees or speciality teas
served in generous pots.

Opening hours: Closed on Tuesdays and on Christmas Day, otherwise
open all year from 10.00am to 6.00pm except for a two-week break
some time in February – so check first. Phone: 01625 576370.

The Route

Leaving the Coffee Tavern, turn left along the road in the direction of Pott Shrigley. After a very short distance turn left again, leaving the surfaced road for a bridleway which climbs steadily towards Birchencliff Farm, a pleasant dwelling surrounded by trees.

Negotiate the stone stile alongside the small pool which belongs to Ryder Brow Fishing Club and continue along the bridleway which, after a short respite, resumes its gradual climb through a landscape of shallow valleys and green, rounded hills.

Beyond the next five-barred gate proceed for 10 metres before turning left into Moorside Lane, another bridleway. After 300 metres, and just before "Keeper's Cottage", turn right onto a footpath signed to Kettleshulme and Bowstones. This continues upwards to the right of a partially collapsed drystone wall until it reaches a makeshift gate between the end of a fence and a wall on Planted Moor.

Keep to the same line for 100 metres until the path is joined by another coming in from the right. From this junction maintain direction along the edge of Bakestonedale Moor as the wide path undulates for approximately one mile.

Over the wall on your left is the upper moor of Lyme Park where a

The Coffee Tavern – with its welcoming sign

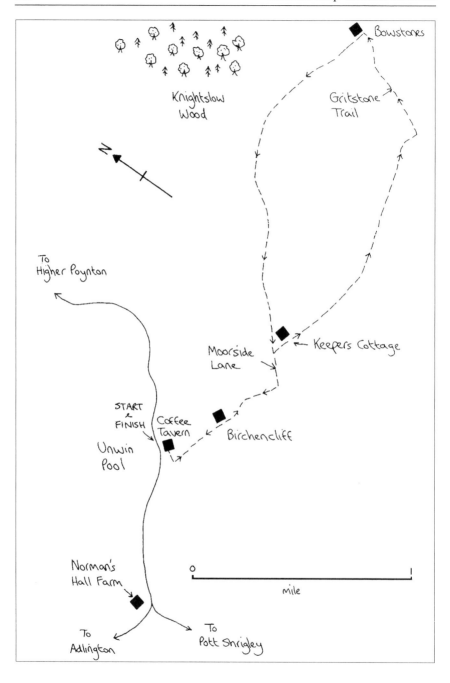

large herd of red deer is often to be seen at close hand. To the right there is an extensive panorama towards the Cheshire Plain and the Triangulation Pillar on Sponds Hill confirms that you have reached a height of 410 metres above sea level.

After passing to the left of a small brick wall with concrete culverts set into it, negotiate another gate before crossing about 150 metres of boggy ground to meet a bridleway. This traverses the high moors from Brink Farm on the Pott Shrigley to Whaley Bridge road to Bowstonegate and forms part of the Gritstone Trail.

Turn left along this until negotiating a five-barred gate by Bowstones Farm. This stretch of the route offers some splendid views out over the Goyt Valley to Kinder Scout and South Head. Through the gate, and where the rough surface ends, turn left over a stile. With the Bowstones and Bowstones Farm on your right, advance to a second stile.

Stay with the well-worn path as it descends the rough moorland until meeting a ladder stile alongside a five-barred gate at the entrance to Knightslow Wood. Do not negotiate the stile. Turn left along another broad track which dips slightly to cross a stream before climbing a little and then traversing a level stretch of moorland for a considerable distance until reaching a stile.

Over this the path develops into a wide track, Moorside Lane. Proceed beyond Moorside Farm, a short distance to your right, until reaching "Keeper's Cottage". From there retrace your outward steps to the Coffee Tavern.

Walk 23. Poynton

Route: Higher Poynton – Haresteads Farm – Throstle Nest – Green Farm – Lockgate Farm – Macclesfield Canal – Poynton Coppice – Higher Poynton.

Start: Nelson Pit Visitor Centre, Lyme Road, Higher Poynton. Map reference 940835.

Distance: 4½ miles.

Map: "Wilmslow, Macclesfield & Congleton", no. 268 in the O.S. Explorer series.

Public Transport: The start is served by frequent daily (including Sunday) buses from Manchester and Stockport.

By Car: The start may be reached by a minor road from the A523 in the centre of Poynton village or from Pott Shrigley, turning right at Norman's Hall Farm. The car park is by the Visitor Centre, just a short distance along the road opposite to the Boar's Head.

The Tea Shop

Since the previous edition, the Lyme View Café has closed. However, there is a choice of places for refreshments, all very close to each other:

Firstly, there is the 'Original Coffee Tavern' next door to the Boar's Head. This is the only 'tea shop' in the immediate area and it serves teas, coffees, ice creams and a range of snacks. Closed on Mondays.

Next, the Boar's Head itself: known for its ales and traditional pub-style meals. Normal pub opening hours. Handy if want a substantial meal.

Finally, the "Trading Post" – a little shop-cum-café with outdoor seating alongside the canal, just a short distance from the canal bridge. Plastic cups and prepacked snacks. Day boat hire in case you fancy a cruise.

Nelson Pit Visitor Centre

Don't just dash out of the car park to start your walk: call in at the Visitor Centre to learn about the area in general, and Poynton in particular. Both young and old will enjoy finding out about the past, thanks to the well-designed displays. There is an excellent selection of leaflets about nearby attractions. Note also that there are toilets here.

Higher Poynton: The Macclesfield Canal

The Macclesfield Canal

This canal forms a link between the Peak Forest Canal at Marple in Greater Manchester, and the Trent and Mersey Canal at Kidsgrove in Staffordshire, a distance of 26 miles.

It shares with the Peak Forest Canal the distinction of being the highest navigable waterway in England. It passes over the nearby town of Bollington by means of a spectacular aqueduct and at Bosley, to the south of Macclesfield, there is an impressive flight of 12 locks.

In its heyday it transported stone from nearby quarries, coal from the mines at Poynton and textiles from Macclesfield and Bollington. The Macclesfield Canal is reputed to have formed the cornerstone of Pickfords' transport business. The canal eventually declined with the opening of a railway line between Macclesfield and Marple. In recent years the towpath has been improved by British Waterways and Macclesfield Borough Council for use by walkers.

The Middlewood Way

This special walking route was opened by Stockport Metropolitan Borough Council and Macclesfield Borough Council in 1985. It runs along the track of the former railway line which linked Macclesfield with Rose Hill, Marple.

It is about 11 miles long and has many access points. Horse riding and cycling are also permitted and there is a cycle hire centre operated by the Macclesfield Groundwork Trust in Bollington.

Poynton

During the eighteenth and nineteenth centuries Poynton was the centre of a thriving coal mining industry with several small mines on or near the canal and railway. In later years it became noted for the quality of the bricks manufactured there. Now it is mainly residential.

The Route

Turn left from the Visitor Centre and walk uphill, soon crossing the canal bridge. Stay forward along the rough track to reach a cattle grid by a white house on your left. A short distance beyond this a Y-junction is reached. Take the right-hand track to maintain direction, originally staying close to the wood on your right where the silver birch are festooned with small bracket fungus.

Negotiate a small wicket gate to the right of another cattle grid and pass through open pastoral countryside before embarking on a gentle descent to a gate alongside a third cattle grid where a culverted stream is crossed.

From this point the track begins a gentle climb to Haresteads Farm. By the first corner of the farmhouse turn right into the farmyard and then immediately make another right turn to a wicket gate. Through that, turn sharply to the left, walking alongside a corrugated metal building on your left. Where that ends continue forward to the right of a wire fence and down a very short stretch of rough pasture to a wooden stile. Over this there follows a very short climb through a clump of trees to the skeleton of a disintegrating wooden hut already swamped by vegetation.

By this turn right to reach a stile after 75 metres. Continue to the left of a hedge until passing through a gate a few metres before Throstle Nest Farm. Swing right to a small waymarked gate after a few metres and then follow the signs around the outside of the buildings and garden, which are on your left, until emerging into a small field by means of a stile.

Turn left, still to the right of the farm and, with a hedge on your left, round the first field corner. In the second corner negotiate a stile, turn left again and, still staying close to that hedge on your left, advance a further 20 metres to another stile which provides access to a wide track.

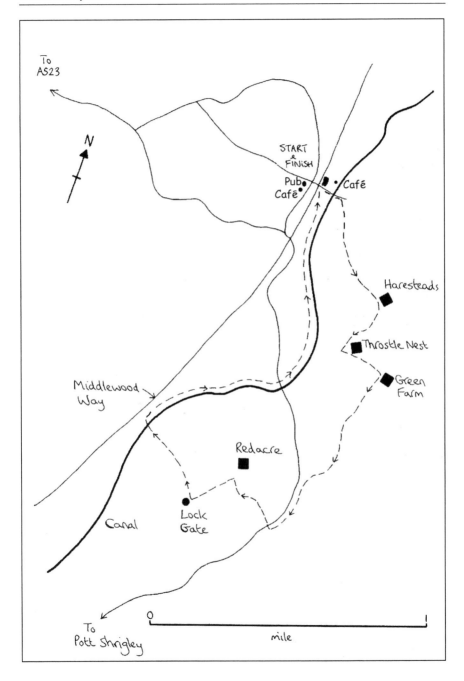

This tortuous navigation avoids a straightforward but forbidden route through the farmyard.

Turn right along the track, climbing to Green Farm. By the first corner of the farmhouse turn right to join a broad track which is signed a few metres beyond the house. By a small pond on your right, this track twists through a Z-bend and over a cattle grid before straightening to continue its course to another cattle grid and descending to pass to the right of West Park Gate Farm.

Cross a stone bridge and ignore a signed path to the right. Remain with the track until it emerges onto the Pott Shrigley road by Green Close Methodist Church. Turn left, climbing for approximately 100 metres until the road levels. After a similar distance and a few metres before a white house, turn right by a footpath sign into Simpson's Lane which descends by a cottage which takes its name from the bridleway.

Continue beyond this cottage but a short distance before reaching the impressive buildings of Redacres Hall Farm, and by a telegraph pole, turn left over a stile which has "To Lockgate Farm" painted on it in white letters.

The clear, unmistakable path worms its way across the field, heading for the left-hand corner of Lockgate Farm. There, turn right over a stile, and staying to the right of the farm buildings, advance to a second waymarked stile which is followed by a lane.

Continue along this for more than a quarter of a mile until it crosses over the Macclesfield Canal by a hump-backed bridge by Woods Lane Marina (Adlington Basin).

You now have a choice of route. Canal lovers can turn right along the towpath of the Macclesfield Canal and return to the starting point.

The alternative is to for a few yards and turn right along the Middlewood Way. Eventually this will lead you through the car park at Poynton Coppice and then to the site of the former railway station at Higher Poynton. This is now a picnic site and is opposite to the Boar's Head.

Walk 24. Styal

Route: Quarry Bank Mill – Norcliffe Chapel – Willow Cottage – Golf Course – Clay Lane – Linney's Bridge – Quarry Bank Mill.

Start: The car park, Quarry Bank Mill and Styal Country Park. Map reference 835831.

Distance: 3½ miles

Map: "Wilmslow, Macclesfield & Congleton", no. 268 in the O.S. Explorer series.

Public Transport: Styal is served by frequent daily buses from Wilmslow and Manchester Airport. Some trains from Manchester, Wilmslow and Alderley Edge stop at Styal station.

By Car: Styal Country Park and Quarry Bank Mill are off the B5166 Wilmslow to Gatley road. The mill and country park are both signed from the A34 north of Wilmslow and also from Junction 6 of the M56. There is a large car park.

The Tea Shop

There are at least three possibilities based on Quarry Bank Mill:

A pleasant DIY option is to have a picnic on the Mill meadow.

Alternatively, for a quick drink, snack (including sandwiches and cakes) or ice-cream, try the Mill Pantry in the mill yard. In addition to tea and coffee, the hot chocolate is highly recommended. Open daily, (except Mondays, between October and mid-March). Enthusiastic volunteers and a range of secondhand books to browse through and/or purchase.

For a more substantial meal, there is the Mill Restaurant (licensed) off the mill yard. Children's menu available during school holidays.

Opening hours: in general – March to September, Monday to Sunday, 10.30am to 5.00pm; October to March, Tuesday to Friday 10.30am to 4.00pm; Saturdays and Sundays, 10.30am to 4.30pm; Closed on Christmas Day and on Mondays during the winter. The website www.nationaltrust.org.uk has up-to-date information, or phone: 01625 527468.

Quarry Bank Mill

Now regarded as one of the finest working museums in the country,

Norcliffe Chapel, Styal

Quarry Bank Mill, Styal, was built by Samuel Gregg in the late eighteenth century with additions in early part of the nineteenth. It is typical of the early mills of the Industrial Revolution with its weaving sheds
and warehouses.

Constructed in the Georgian style with a distinctive cupola, it sits
alongside the River Bollin which provided the power that drove the
spinning machines and looms. A special village with its own church,
shop and school was built to house the workers. There was also an Apprentice House for the very young pauper children brought from London. The mill, surrounding woodlands, village and Apprentice House
are now owned by the National Trust which has restored the mill, including the giant water wheel, to working order.

Opening hours: April to the end of September, Daily, 11.00 a.m. to 5.00
p.m; October to March, daily (except Monday) 11.00 a.m. to 4.00 p.m.

The Route

Leave the car park to the left of the entrance which, 10 metres beyond
the payment kiosk, reaches the main approach drive to the mill. (This is
forbidden to unauthorised traffic).

Turn right along this for a few metres but, by a large oak tree and a National Trust sign which reads, "Styal To The Woods", turn left onto an excellent maintained path which runs just to the left of a hedge.

Pass through two stiles until meeting a wider track by an information panel on the boundary of the North Woods. Turn right, this new path staying just inside the woodland boundary until it exits by two squeezer stiles in quick succession.

Stay forward to pass to the right of the Norcliffe Chapel. According to the deeds of the trust establishing this place of worship it was built "for the worship of God and the furtherance of Christian Life free from the fetters of any written or unwritten declarations of faith". It is open every Sunday from Easter to the end of September between 2.30 p.m. and 5.00 p.m.

Continue beyond the chapel and the subsequent lychgate to the remnants of the medieval cross which used to stand by the village green. After being damaged as the result of a road accident it was transferred to its present location.

By the cross turn left into the cobbled lane leading to an intersection in front of a row of redbrick cottages. There turn right so the cottages are on your left. By the last one keep the same line of direction between two hedges until meeting the road from Styal to Altrincham.

Cross to the facing wooden stile and footpath sign. Over the stile turn sharply to the left along the clearly defined path as it passes through a gateway some 50 metres to the right of a field corner. Once through that gateway turn sharply to the right to pass beneath some overhead wires to a stile. Maintain direction, still with a hedge on your right, to the B5166, the road from Wilmslow to Gatley.

Cross to the footpath sign opposite and follow your general line of direction by walking through the wide gap to the right of "Willow Cottage" to reach a stile after 20 metres which is quickly followed by a wooden kissing gate.

Cross the railway line by means of the footbridge to a second kissing gate which allows access to Styal golf course. Cross this by maintaining a straight line immediately to the right of a line of trees and shrubs and guided by a succession of waymarker poles until reaching a wooden seat by a small pond. Cross the surfaced road and stay to the right of a row of hawthorns for 50 metres to sign reading "Next Tee". Negotiate the stile to the right of this to exit from the golf course.

Stay to the right of a hedge for 40 metres before turning left over a wooden stile and then sharp right so maintaining the general line of direction to the left of a hedge.

On your left there is a large clump of dead trees rising out of a dried-up pond, the remnants of one of the many marl pits scattered over the Cheshire Plain. Marl was used extensively for spreading over land when it was ploughed, not to mention forming the basis of a good cricket pitch.

Negotiate a stile in the facing hedge by the field corner and then veer about 20 degrees to the left, aiming for an obvious stile in the hedge ahead.

Over that veer 45 degrees to the left, heading towards a stile in the next field corner. After this follow the well-defined path across a large open area of scrub consisting principally of scattered hawthorns, rosebay willowherb and tall grass.

At the first intersection of paths, after a distance of only 50 metres, continue forwards for a further 200 metres until meeting a second intersection. A few metres beyond this is a stile by an oak tree in a facing hedge. Ignore this stile. Instead, at the intersection, turn right to walk close to the hedge on your left. After 250 metres pass through a pair of old stone gateposts and, keeping "The Grange" on your left, advance until meeting Clay Lane.

Turn right. Initially this is surfaced and has bungalows on your left. However, beyond the final bungalow it reverts to a narrow, partially hedged lane.

Pass to the right of a metal five-barred gate carrying a "NO ENTRY" sign to reach an inverted Y-junction. Bear right to meet the Handforth to Styal road by Southfield Manor, now a nursing home. Turn right but, after 100 metres, go left over a wooden stile onto the path signed to Linney's Bridge. Stay to the left of the fence but, in the first field corner, make a right turn over a stile as the narrow path runs between wire fences.

Eventually it enters a small wood and winds its course between the trees to a Y-junction with a footpath finger post close to the road at Linney's Bridge.

Do not emerge onto the road. Turn right over a waymarked stile to follow a path signed to Quarry Bank Mill. Cross a small field, veering uphill and to the right to a wooden stile.

Continue to the left of a fence before curving left by a hawthorn tree and an elder to another stile. From this point continue along the boundary of the woods, following a line above a small wooded clough which is on your left.

In due course, the path swings left over a wooden footbridge to a

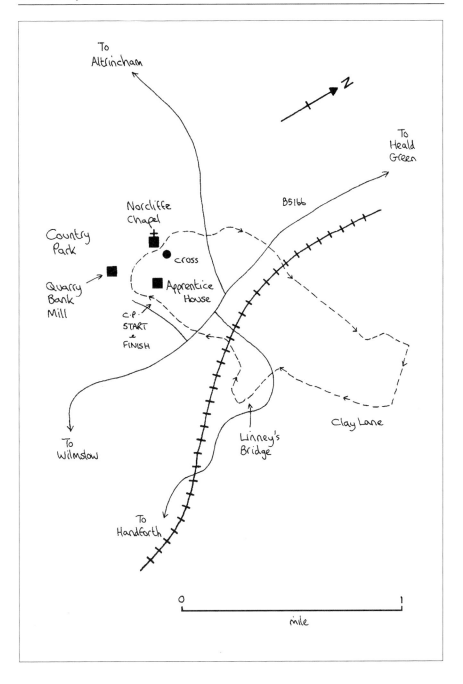

To
Altrincham

Z

To
Heald
Green

Norcliffe
Chapel

B5166

Country
Park

● cross

Quarry
Bank
Mill

Apprentice
House

C.P.
START
&
FINISH

Clay Lane

To
Wilmslow

Linney's
Bridge

To
Handforth

0   1

mile

waymarked stile. Beyond that, stay forward over a field while aiming for a stile located by the left-hand corner of a bungalow.

Proceed alongside this bungalow to a wooden footpath sign. Turn left over the railway footbridge and left again at the far side. Walk to the right of a hedge to another footpath sign. Turn right along the wide track by Wilmslow Albion Football Club's ground until emerging onto the B5166. Turn left along this for 10 metres and then go right into the approach road to Styal Country Park and Quarry Bank Mill.

To reach the Mill Kitchen keep the car park on your left before descending the slope to the mill complex.

Walk 25. Knutsford

Route: Knutsford – Tatton Mere – Old Hall – Tatton Hall – Melchett Mere – Tatton Mere – Knutsford.

Start: The car park off King Street, Knutsford. Map reference 753786.

Distance: 6 miles.

Maps: "Wilmslow, Macclesfield & Congleton", no. 268 in the O.S. Explorer series.

Public Transport: Knutsford is served by frequent daily (including Sunday) trains from Chester, Northwich, Altrincham, Stockport and Manchester Piccadilly.

There are daily buses from Chester, Northwich, Altrincham, Warrington, Wilmslow (not Sunday) and Macclesfield (not Sunday).

By Car: Knutsford is signed from Junction 19 of the M6 Motorway. It is on the A50 between Warrington and Stoke-on-Trent. It may also be reached by the A5033 from Northwich, the A537 from Macclesfield and the B5085 from Wilmslow and Alderley Edge.

The Tea Shop

If you arrive at the Courtyard Coffee House, King Street, Knutsford by Penny Farthing you are entitled to claim a free tea but, sadly, walkers have to pay. It would be true to say that this antique but romantic form of transport provides the theme for this most excellent of tea shops because inside there is a suspended display of about thirty of these two-wheeled machines. Another unusual attraction is the miniature American train which runs along the track fixed at the point where the walls and ceiling meet.

Even as you approach the setting is perfect. From King Street you pass through a passageway into a cobbled courtyard which probably existed when Mrs. Gaskell stayed in the town. The Courtyard Coffee House *(pictured on the front cover of this book)* is the epitome of an ideal English tea room. Except at busy periods you can choose whether to sit in the old dining room or in the light and airy conservatory.

The tea, of which several speciality brews are available, is served in large but elegant pots, matched by equally refined crockery. Unusually, too, there is a wide variety of coffees on offer. Amongst the soft drinks is Elderflower Champagne.

The menu matches the atmosphere with all dishes freshly prepared using seasonal ingredients wherever possible. Unusual soups, for example, may be based on fennel and courgette or parsnip and orange. For something really substantial try the Welsh Rarebit, made to a secret recipe.

The cream tea is unrivalled not only in Cheshire but in this country. If it is a scone you want you may have to wait for it to be baked as I have on more than one occasion.

Once tasted, you will never forget the wonderful gateaux which change on a daily basis and tempt the palate with such flavours as candied lemon, chocolate, coffee or carrot.

Opening hours: Mondays to Fridays, 10.00 a.m. to 4.30 p.m; Saturdays and Sundays, 10.00 a.m. to 5.00 p.m; Phone: 01565 653974

Knutsford

Knutsford takes its name from King Canute who is reputed to have forded a stream there. As he removed his boots to empty the water out a

The Angel Hotel, Knutsford

wedding party came by. He wished the happy couple as many children as there were grains of sand falling out of his boots.

This legend has given rise to the custom of "Sanding the Streets" during the annual May Day celebrations. This involves creating designs and patterns by using coloured sands on the pavements.

Mentioned in the Domesday Book, Knutsford has a long and important history but it is best known as the setting for Mrs. Gaskell's novel, "Cranford", and this association between the town and author is perpetuated in monuments and street names. The Tourist Information Centre produces a very useful town guide for anyone wishing to stroll round after their visit to the Courtyard Coffee House.

Tatton

It is worth while to make several breaks in the course of this walk to visit the varied attractions of Tatton. Prehistoric remains have been excavated alongside Tatton Mere by archaeologists from Manchester University. Our route passes the Old Hall, precursor of the present Georgian mansion, home of the Egerton family. Both repay the time spent exploring their interiors. Children may also like to visit the Home Farm.

Full details of all the Tatton attractions along with opening times may be obtained by ringing the Tatton Infoline, (01625) 534435 or the main switchboard on (01625) 534400 or by writing to Administration, Tatton Park, Knutsford, Cheshire, WA16 6QN.

The Route

Take the lower exit from the car park and turn left for 25 metres before making a right turn onto the surfaced path which runs alongside the mere on Knutsford Moor.

This mere is noted as one of the largest areas of fen and reed swamp in Cheshire, containing examples of greater reed mace and tussock sedge. A large bird population embraces Canada geese, mute swans, tufted duck and ruddy duck.

Proceed beyond the mere and the pumping station, under the railway bridge and up to Mobberley Road. Turn left and walk along to the lay-by where you turn left again into Teal Avenue then Mallard Close which ends with a hump-back bridge over the railway line. The entrance to Dog Wood is immediately on your right. Dog Wood is noted locally for its population of wrens, blackbirds, blue tits, great tits and woodpeckers.

A wooden gate provides an entrance into Tatton Park and allows the path to continue alongside Tatton Mere until reaching a jetty. By this, turn right along a wide chatter track for 150 metres to a T-junction in front of a Scout camp site.

Turn left following the track through a large Z bend to pick-up a deer fence on your right as you traverse the open parkland. In late summer and early autumn look for the large flocks of lapwing roosting on the fields beyond this fence. Pass through a five-barred metal gate (this is often left open) to enter an impressive oak plantation, parts of which are used as a car park.

Maintain direction to a T-junction close by some toilets. Turn left down the slope for a distance of about 100 metres and, by the first junction, make a right turn along a surfaced track which is signed to the Old Hall, the Landscape History Trail and the Melchett Walk. (Booklets available from the Gift Shop include "Discover Tatton Park on Foot" and "Wartime Tatton".)

Stay to the right of another car park to pass to the left of the Old Hall. By the far corner of the boundary fence of the Old Hall and a display panel illustrating the story of "Tatton At War", make a sharp left turn onto a broad green path which traverses the parkland and makes for enjoyable walking.

After a considerable distance you will reach a T-junction by the very moving stone memorial to members of the parachute forces who trained at Tatton before heading off to the various theatres of war between 1940 and 1945.

Turn left and follow the clear path, staying to the right of a plantation until meeting the drive from the main entrance to Tatton Hall itself. Turn left towards Tatton Hall but, at the next junction, fork left along the drive signed to the Old Hall (if you wish to visit the Hall, turn right). You do not have to walk on the hard surface but may use the grass parkland on either side.

Eventually you will pass Melchett Mere on your right and, at the junction a short distance beyond, maintain direction towards the Knutsford entrance with Tatton Mere now a short distance away on your left.

At the entrance use the small gate to the right of the cattle grid and proceed through the impressive classical arch. 100 metres beyond, where the road bends to the right, stay forwards along the broad path to meet King Street. Turn left to pass the Courtyard Coffee Shop .

Opposite Mrs Gaskell's Tower turn left into Cotton Shop Yard and, at the far end, emerge into the car park from which you started.

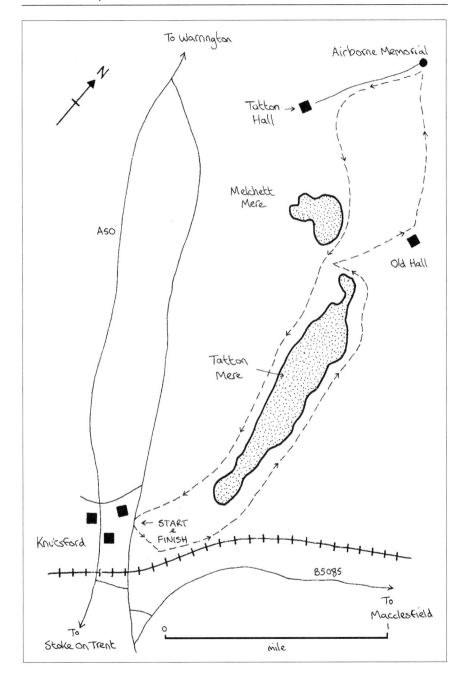

Walk 26. Dunham Massey

Route: Dunham Massey – Brickkiln Lane – Little Bollington – Bridgewater Canal – Dunham Town – Oldfield Lane – Altrincham Golf Course – Charcoal Road – Dunham Massey.

Start: The car park, Dunham Massey Park. Map reference 733875

Distance: 4½ miles.

Maps: 1. "Wilmslow, Macclesfield & Congleton", no. 268 in the O.S. Explorer series. 2. "Bolton, Wigan & Warrington", no. 276 in the O.S. Explorer series.

Public Transport: Frequent daily (including Sunday) buses from Warrington and Altrincham pass the entrance to Dunham Massey Park.

By Car: Leave the M6 at junction 19 and take the A56 in the direction of Altrincham. At the Bowdon traffic lights turn left along the minor road signed to Partington. The entrance to Dunham Massey Park is a further half mile. From Manchester and Altrincham take the A56 Chester Road, turning right at the Bowdon traffic lights. There is a large car park (fee).

The Tea Shop

The Stables Restaurant is located on the upper floor above the shop and is adequately signed from the grounds of Dunham Massey Hall. It is a light, airy and spacious building of unusual length and with beamed ceiling and exposed brick walls. Unusually it has solid wooden tables and chairs to match.

The light lunches include a changing daily selection of dishes plus filled jacket potatoes, rolls with various fillings and soup with roll. There is a wonderful choice of home-made cakes including flapjacks, date and walnut, chocolate sponge, Victoria sponge and coffee sponge. An alternative is to have afternoon tea or scones with jam and cream. A speciality is the Cheshire Cheese and Herb Scone which is so delicious that it will invariably be followed by a second. Another speciality of the house is Dunham Pudding served with either cream or custard. A really fruity concoction, it certainly provides ample energy for the afternoon walker. There is a choice of coffees and a variety of speciality teas, all served in large pots.

Opening hours: Daily, April to October: 11.00 a.m. to 5.00 p.m; November – December: Thursday to Sunday: 11.00 a.m. to 4.00 p.m; January – March: Saturdays and Sundays only: 11.00 a.m. to; 4.00 p.m; Phone: 0161 941 1025

The hall, Dunham Massey

Dunham Massey

This fine Georgian house was the home of the Earls of Stamford until 1976 when it passed into the ownership of the National Trust. It is renowned for its collections of furniture, family portraits and Huguenot silver. Currently extensive work is in hand to restore some of the fine avenues of trees to their original designs. An ancient Jacobean flour mill has been returned to working order. The parkland, which covers 250 acres, supports a fine herd of fallow deer and contains a slaughter house and an unusual deer barn.

The Route

Leave the car park by the main entrance, turning left for some five metres along Charcoal Road. By the footpath sign to Bollington, turn left into Brickkiln Lane which is also signed to Bollington Mill.

Initially this wends its way through woodland with the brick boundary wall of Dunham park on your left but eventually it leaves the trees behind for open country with the River Bollin close by on the right.

By Bollington Mill, now converted into luxury apartments, turn right across the metal footbridge spanning the river and stay forward for a short distance along the very narrow road while passing the unusually named pub, "The Swan With Two Nicks"

Some 50 metres beyond, at a Y-junction, fork right along the cobbled lane signed as part of the Bollin Valley way, a medium distance linear route which follows the course of this Cheshire river from Macclesfield to the Manchester Ship Canal.

Pass under an arched canal bridge before turning immediately to the right to ascend a flight of five stone steps followed by a path onto the towpath of the Bridgewater Canal, where you turn left. Cross the Bollin Aqueduct followed by the bridge over Woodhouse Lane. Ten metres after passing beneath a redbrick, hump-backed bridge, turn left through a wooden kissing gate and left again up the slight slope to Back Lane.

Make another left turn for the short distance to the T-junction by St Mark's Church and opposite the Post Office in Dunham Town. Go right into School Lane but, after a mere ten metres and by a footpath sign, turn left into another lane signed to Oldfield Lane.

Pass to the left of a white cottage, following the lane as it runs to the right of the churchyard to a wooden stile. Over this it is flanked by hedgerows until reaching a three-armed footpath post. Turn right across a field, passing to the right of a solitary tree to a stile with a footpath sign alongside which provides access to Oldfield Lane.

Turn right but, after 20 metres and by another sign, make a left turn. Cross another field to a sign with four arms. Turn left along the path signed to Altrincham, staying close to the hedge on your left until the first stile provides an entry onto Altrincham Golf Course.

Taking your direction from the arm of the footpath finger post, veer slightly to the right across the links until meeting a broad track by tee number 7. Turn left along the track for a short distance until reaching a brown footpath notice attached to a tree. At this junction make an acute right turn onto a narrow path and, passing to the right of a small car park, reach Charcoal Road.

Cross diagonally right to a very conspicuous and large white gate with an extremely tall ladder stile alongside. Over this it is possible to follow the surfaced driveway for approximately one mile if you wish to head directly back to Dunham Hall. However, a more interesting alternative is to fork left almost immediately beyond the stile, taking the well-worn grass path and staying with it until it forms a T-junction with a similar path flanked by an avenue of tall trees. Turn right along this to walk by the deer paddocks on your way back to the Hall and the Stables Restaurant.

After refreshments turn left and left again under the archway to cross the moat before turning right for the short distance to the car park.

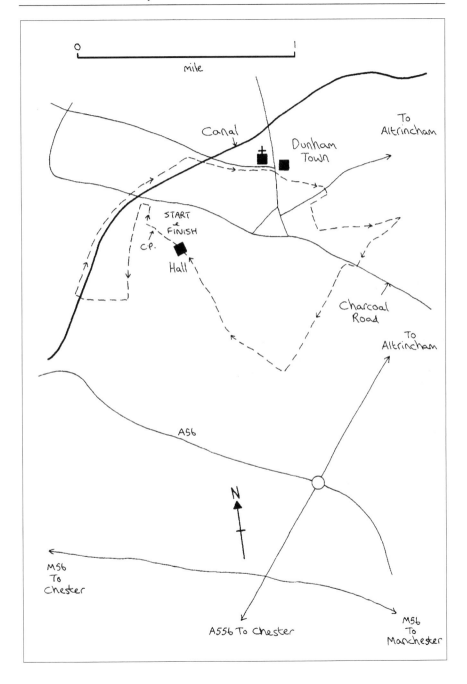

Walk 27. Lymm

Route: Lymm Library – Lymm Dam – The Avenue – Booth's Lane – Mersey Brook Lane – Bridgewater Canal – Lymm Library.

Start: The car park by Lymm Library. Map reference 681874

Distance: 3½ miles.

Map: "Bolton, Wigan & Warrington", no. 276 in the O.S. Explorer series.

Public Transport: Lymm is served by frequent daily (including Sundays) buses from Warrington and Altrincham.

By Car: Lymm is on the A56 which runs from Junction 7 of the M56 Motorway to Warrington. It is also signed from the M6 at Junction 20. The library car park is signed from the A56.

The Tea Shop

Refreshments are now available at Sexton's Bakery and Café at 2, Eagle Brow in the centre of Lymm village. The quality of the fare on offer may be gauged by the fact that Philip Sexton is the fifth generation of a family of bakers. The present business was established in Lymm in 1969 but there was a major refurbishment including the addition of a café in 1997.

As you enter the premises there is an enticing smell of freshly-baked bread and the appetite will be further sharpened by the sight of the large array of cakes and gateaux on display. In addition there is a discerning selection of English and Continental cheeses in the delicatessen section along with some fine-looking roast hams and other cooked meats. There are also some unusual patés, including wild boar and ginger.

The modern wooden tables and chairs are spread discreetly around the shop and the seating is further supplemented by a small bar with tall stools. There is a fine Welsh dresser with a display of preserves and pickles.

The light meals on offer include a Cheese Platter, a Café Sandwich with a variety of fillings and Ploughman's Lunch. You may select a freshly buttered Croissant or any of the meat or fruit pies, cakes and scones displayed in the bakery section. All may be accompanied by cups of freshly ground coffee or speciality tea or soft drink.

The speciality of the house is its French bread made on the premises from scratch. It is not baked from frozen dough but from French flour specially chosen by Philip.

Opening hours: Monday to Saturday, all year, 9.30 am to 4.30 pm. Closed Sundays.

Lymm

Lymm is an attractive village clustered around its ancient market cross and stocks and nestling beneath the parish church with its pinnacled tower. Once a centre of fustian manufacture, it is dominated by the Bridgewater Canal, now used by pleasure boats but initially the main commercial artery of the Industrial Revolution in the North West of England.

One of Lymm's attractions is the Dingle, a gorge 100 feet deep overhung with foliage and approached from the centre of the village.

The Route

Descend through the car park towards the canal. By the Boat Stage veer right down the cobbles to Bridgewater Street. Turn right but, at the far end turn left into Eagle Brow. Within a few metres, and immediately before the road bridge, turn right into the Dingle, passing a footpath sign after about 50 metres.

Continue along the path through this wooded glen, its steeply sloping sides festooned with ivy, staying to the right of the green railings and Bradley Brook. Where the railings corner away to the left notice the waterfall under the arch of the road bridge. Climb the steps to reach the A56. Cross directly to the footpath sign and take the path alongside Lymm Dam which is on your left.

Attempts to landscape it on a grand design by Lord Leverhulme were abandoned but there are still relics of the aborted enterprise along our route. By the first corner of the dam, turn right onto a signed footpath which runs along the west bank through a mixture of deciduous trees. Beyond a wooden bench, while the reservoir curves away to the left, the path pursues its onward course but the two meet again shortly before a wooden barrier with a notice board and footpath sign adjacent.

Through the barrier an intersection is reached. Look to the left to see the ornamental bridge, part of the Leverhulme grand design. However, make a right turn at this intersection to reach a road after ten metres. Turn left along The Avenue which, in the French fashion, is lined on both sides with Lombardy poplars so, in the middle of Cheshire, creating a continental landscape.

Bridgewater Canal, Lymm

At the far end of The Avenue turn right along the B5158, using the grass verge and then the pavement and passing Turner's Pool on your left. 100 metres beyond the 30 mph signs make a left turn into Booth's Lane. After some 200 metres, and beyond the last house, turn right by the footpath sign to follow a path which runs between a wire fence on the left and a series of garden fences on the right.

Ahead is a wide-ranging view of the Mersey Valley and beyond into South Lancashire with Thelwall Viaduct conspicuous closer to hand. How pleasant it is to be travelling at a snail's pace on foot rather than hurtling along the M6 Motorway in a tin box at 70 mph. This advantage certainly allows time for spotting the small tortoiseshell butterflies and the many pheasants hereabouts.

On reaching a T-junction with a three-armed footpath post make a left turn to walk between two barbed wire fences. After a wooden squeezer stile keep to the boundary of a large field with a hedge on the left. 50 metres before reaching a conspicuous waymarked stile, and by a footpath sign, turn right over a wooden footbridge and stile to walk immediately to the left of a hedge until a further stile permits entry onto Massey Brook Lane with the Bridgewater Canal facing you.

Turn right along Massey Brook Lane, keeping to the pavement until the junction with the A56. Turn left along Camsley Lane, as the A56 is

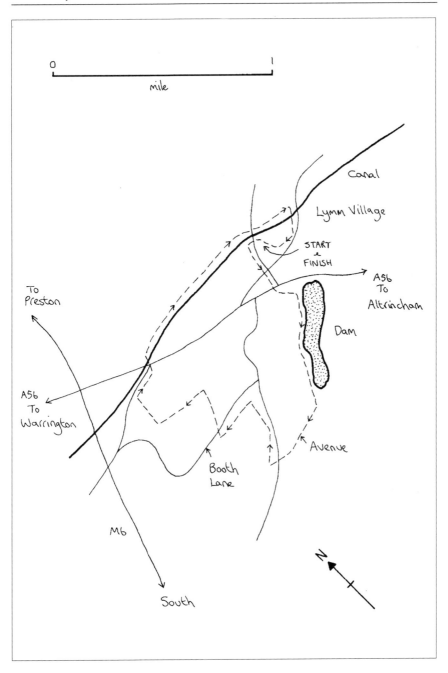

known at this point, and cross the concrete bridge spanning the Bridgewater Canal. At the far end turn right down the cobbled Yeald Brow and then maintain direction along the canal towpath. Enterprising householders on both sides of the water have utilised the canalside for hen runs, lawns and small strips of flower or vegetable gardens.

After approximately one mile the canal passes beneath Brookfield Bridge. Continue further along the towpath until reaching the hump-backed Lymm Bridge. Immediately before this turn left through a small metal gate and proceed in front of a row of cottages to New Road.

Turn right, re-crossing the canal to enter The Cross. Descend the hill to pass the actual cross on your left before swinging right over another bridge to enter Eagle Brow. After 10 metres, and by Barclay's Bank, turn right into Bridgewater Street for a few metres before veering left by the Post Office to climb to the canal and the boat stage. There, turn left for the final few metres to your starting point.

Walk 28. Wilmslow

Route: Moor Lane – Lindow Moss – Saltersley – Morley Green – Newgate – Moor Lane

Start: Ned Yates Garden Centre, Moor Lane, Wilmslow. Map ref: SJ823802

Distance: 4½ miles

Map: "Wilmslow, Macclesfield & Congleton", no. 268 in the O.S. Explorer series.

Public Transport: regular buses from Wilmslow town centre.

By Car: From the town centre, drive along Water Lane and turn left at The Nose, down Hawthorn Street. Turn right at the Carter's Arms along Chapel Lane, which becomes Moor Lane. At the end of Moor Lane, keep right and you soon come to the garden centre – there is a sign to direct you. Most times you can park in the garden centre car park while you complete your walk (please ask first); if not, park considerately on the road.

The Tea Shop

Ned Yates Garden Centre is tucked away in the south-west corner of Wilmslow, at the end of Moor Lane. The café is behind the shop and open-air seating is available in the summertime. Inside, the atmosphere is cosy and there is a small selection of scones, carrot cake and toasted teacakes, plus ice-creams. Opening hours: weekdays 9.00 – 5.30, weekends 9.30 – 5.30. From February to October closing time is 4.30pm.

The Walk

A sketch map is not provided for this walk, as it is very easy to follow from the text alone. If in doubt, take an OS map!

Continue beyond the garden centre in the same direction as you arrived. After a short distance, the lane bears right – ignore the track on your left. After a total of about five minutes, the lane bears left and – just before Lindow Court Park – you turn right through a gate. Continue along the footpath for 70m, then turn right at a waymark through a break in the hedge. Cross a field to a concrete footbridge and you are now in the bizarre landscape of Lindow Moss. Although the peat workings are undeniably ugly, they provide a habitat for many species of birds and both silver birch and heather flourish on the acidic soil.

Continue straight ahead, crossing footbridges as necessary (these may change as peat working progresses). Ignore turns to the left or right until a more substantial bridge heads off to the left. Cross this to an area thick with bracken and pass a small private nature reserve on your left. Go through an avenue of silver birch and you reach a track which serves Saltersley Hall – an ancient building that was, in the 19th century, a staging post for packhorse trains carrying salt from Northwich to Yorkshire. In the 1980s you could have bought afternoon tea from an elderly Mrs Croxall; many such farmhouses used to offer refreshments to weary walkers, prior to draconian EU health regulations.

Turn right along the track and, after 80m, turn left (footpath sign). Cross the stile and continue with the hedge on your left to another footpath sign. Turn right here and you will soon see a large fishing lake, formed as the result of sand extraction; in the course of this the original footpath was flooded and a long battle ensued to establish the pleasant path along which you are now walking. Follow the path, keeping the lake on your right, to the extreme end of the lake. Cross a stile and turn left along the track, passing bungalows to both left and right.

At a cross-roads, turn left along a lane signed as `Bridle Path to Morley'. Where the tarmac surface bends right to a gateway, keep straight on along a track which emerges onto Eccups Lane. Follow this to the main road, turn right and then – after 50m, turn right again down a signposted track. This leads straight ahead, through a rural backwater that seems a million miles away from the hustle of Wilmslow. Just keep walking and eventually you emerge from woodland into an open grassy area which is, surprisingly, a reclaimed landfill site. Continue up and over a slight hill to a T-junction of paths. Turn left here and walk for about 200m, passing behind the waste-disposal site – currently closed but it may reopen, depending on local politics. In case you were wondering, the metal flues that you can see around here are to assist in burning off excess methane from the decaying waste. This avoids having the whole lot blowing up, which might detract from the enjoyment of your imminent afternoon tea.

Just before a wooded area, turn right and follow the path to the left of a Colditz-style wire fence around the waste site – currently closed but it may reopen, depending on local politics. Go through a metal gate and turn left at the road to walk along Newgate. After 100m, turn right (footpath sign) along a grassy track. You are now back in the Lindow area, though not yet with peat extraction. There are, however, many paths to follow – and to get lost on – so follow these directions carefully: at the first intersection you reach, turn right along a wider track, passing some tumble-down stables. Continue for 300m or so, passing a house on the right. Ignore the first track on your left – instead, bear right and continue for another 150m to a clear T-junction; this is where you turn left. It's easy from here: continue all the way along this track, passing alongside a gate, to a tarmac road; at a more major road, turn right and you're almost back to your car – and the prospect of morning coffee or afternoon tea should spur you on.

Also of interest:

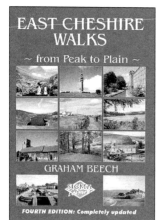